DJANGO 5.1.X FOR WEB DEVELOPMENT

Transform Your Web Development Skills With Django 5.1.x

KRISTINE ELLIS

Chapter 1: Introduction to Django 5.1.x

What is Django? A Brief History and Evolution

Django is a high-level Python web framework designed to promote **rapid development, clean code, and pragmatic design choices**. It provides an organized and efficient way to build scalable web applications while following best practices for security and performance. Since its inception, Django has become one of the most widely used frameworks for web development, powering sites like **Instagram, Pinterest, Mozilla, National Geographic, and Disqus**.

The framework was first released in **2005** by **Adrian Holovaty and Simon Willison**, two developers working at a **news organization** called the Lawrence Journal-World. Their goal was to create a **robust and reusable framework** to handle the complex needs of a modern, data-driven website. What they built became Django, named after **Django Reinhardt**, a famous jazz guitarist known for his fast and elegant playing style—an analogy to how Django simplifies web development.

Since its initial release, Django has continuously evolved, introducing **new features and enhancements** to keep up with the demands of modern web applications. Let's take a look at Django's progression over the years.

Key Milestones in Django's Evolution

- **2005** – The first public release of Django (**0.90**).
- **2008** – Django **1.0** is released, introducing stability and a refined API.
- **2012** – Django **1.4** adds support for time zone-aware datetime objects.
- **2015** – Django **1.8** receives long-term support (LTS), solidifying its enterprise use.
- **2017** – Django **2.0** is released, dropping support for Python 2 and embracing Python 3.
- **2020** – Django **3.0** introduces **async capabilities**, making it more suitable for real-time applications.
- **2022** – Django **4.0** improves database indexes and performance tuning.
- **2024-2025** – Django **5.1.x** refines asynchronous support, ORM optimizations, and security updates.

Django has come a long way from a simple framework built for news organizations to a **powerhouse framework used in production by global-scale companies**.

Why Choose Django? Strengths and Use Cases

Django remains a dominant force in web development because of its ability to provide developers with a **fully equipped, production-ready environment**. Here's why Django is preferred by many developers and businesses:

1. Batteries-Included Framework

Django follows the **"batteries-included" philosophy**, meaning it comes with **everything you need to build a web application**—without requiring extra third-party libraries. Built-in features include:

- **Django ORM** – Simplifies database interactions.
- **Django Admin Panel** – A ready-to-use admin interface.
- **Authentication System** – Secure user login and registration.
- **Form Handling** – Easily manage form submissions and validation.
- **Security Middleware** – Protects against common web vulnerabilities.
- **URL Routing & Templating Engine** – Organizes application logic efficiently.

This **full-stack approach** allows developers to focus on building applications rather than setting up infrastructure.

2. Scalability and Performance

Django is used by high-traffic sites such as **Instagram and Mozilla**, proving that it is highly **scalable**. It can handle **millions of users** by leveraging **database optimization techniques**, **caching strategies**, and **asynchronous processing**.

Key scalability features include:

- **Load Balancing** – Works efficiently with **multiple application servers**.
- **Asynchronous Support** – Django **5.1.x** enhances real-time capabilities.
- **Built-in Caching** – Integrates with **Redis, Memcached, and CDN services**.

These features ensure that Django applications perform well under high traffic loads.

3. Security Best Practices

Security is a **core focus** in Django. It provides **built-in protections** against:

- **SQL Injection** – Using ORM to prevent malicious queries.

2

- **Cross-Site Scripting (XSS)** – Automatic escaping in templates.
- **Cross-Site Request Forgery (CSRF)** – CSRF protection enabled by default.
- **Clickjacking Protection** – Built-in middleware for security headers.

Unlike some frameworks that require **third-party plugins** for security, Django has security **built-in and actively maintained** by a dedicated security team.

4. Rapid Development and Clean Code

Django's design principles emphasize:

- **"Don't Repeat Yourself" (DRY)** – Encourages code **reusability**.
- **"Convention Over Configuration"** – Sensible defaults minimize setup.
- **Well-structured MVC/MTV Pattern** – Separates logic and presentation cleanly.

This **developer-friendly approach** makes Django a **great choice for startups, enterprises, and rapid prototyping**.

5. Strong Community and Documentation

Django has one of the **best documentations in the industry**. Whether you are a **beginner or an expert**, the official Django docs and **thousands of community-driven resources** ensure that **help is always available**.

Community support includes:

- **Django's official documentation** – Comprehensive and up to date.
- **Django Forums, Stack Overflow, and GitHub** – Active discussion platforms.
- **Django Packages** – Thousands of reusable Django apps.

A strong community ensures that Django **continues to improve and adapt** to new industry trends.

Where is Django Used? Real-World Applications

Django powers a **wide range of applications**, from **small startups to massive enterprise solutions**.

1. Social Media and Content Platforms

- **Instagram** – Uses Django to handle millions of daily users.

3

- **Pinterest** – Started with Django before expanding its stack.

Django is **perfect for social media apps** because of its ability to handle **large-scale databases, complex relationships, and real-time updates**.

2. News & Media Websites

- **The Washington Post**
- **The Guardian**
- **National Geographic**

Since Django was originally built for news websites, it **excels in content management** and is used by some of the **largest media companies** today.

3. E-Commerce and Marketplace Platforms

- **PrestaShop**
- **Shopify (some internal services)**
- **Disqus**

Django's **secure authentication system, ORM, and built-in caching** make it a **great choice for e-commerce applications**.

4. Finance and Banking Applications

- **Robinhood (early versions used Django)**
- **Banking and fintech startups**

With **high security, performance, and scalability**, Django is **trusted by financial institutions** for building safe web applications.

5. Government and Research Institutions

- **NASA (Some internal tools)**
- **US Library of Congress**

Django's **stability, maintainability, and open-source nature** make it **suitable for government projects and research institutions**.

Django is a **powerful, secure, and scalable** framework that has stood the test of time. With **Django 5.1.x**, the framework continues to evolve, providing developers with **modern tools for building fast, efficient, and robust web applications**.

Its combination of **rapid development, built-in security, and a strong community** makes it a **top choice for web development today**. Whether you are building **a small business website, a large-scale social media platform, or an enterprise API**, Django provides the **best tools** to get the job done efficiently.

Key Features of Django 5.1.x (What's New)

Django 5.1.x introduces **significant improvements** to the framework, focusing on **performance, security, database management, and asynchronous capabilities**. As Django continues to evolve, the 5.1.x release refines many of its existing features while introducing new enhancements that make web development **faster, safer, and more scalable**.

Let's take a **deep dive** into the most notable updates in Django 5.1.x.

1. Enhanced Asynchronous Support

Django has been **gradually adopting asynchronous capabilities** over the past few versions, and Django 5.1.x improves upon this by optimizing support for **async views, database queries, and middleware**.

- **Async Views & Middleware** – Developers can now build **fully asynchronous request/response cycles**, improving performance when handling high-concurrency workloads.
- **Async Database Queries** – Although Django's ORM is still predominantly synchronous, Django 5.1.x **enhances database operations** to support limited async queries, making it easier to integrate with async-compatible database drivers.
- **WebSockets & Real-Time Features** – Django **Channels** (an extension of Django) has received better integration, allowing developers to build real-time applications such as **live chat systems, stock tickers, and collaborative tools**.

This update is particularly beneficial for **high-traffic applications**, reducing request-processing time and making Django a more competitive option for building **real-time services**.

5

2. Improved ORM Performance & Query Optimization

Django's ORM (Object-Relational Mapper) is one of its strongest features, allowing developers to interact with databases using Python instead of raw SQL. Django 5.1.x **refines ORM performance** with:

- **Automatic Query Optimization** – The framework **intelligently reduces redundant queries**, improving speed when fetching related objects.
- **Asynchronous Query Support (Limited)** – While full async ORM support is still under development, **some read operations now support async execution**, improving database performance under heavy loads.
- **Faster Aggregation Queries** – Optimized handling of **sum, count, and average** operations, reducing execution time for large datasets.

For applications that rely heavily on **database interactions**, these improvements provide noticeable speed gains.

3. Native Support for JSONField in All Databases

Django 5.1.x **officially supports JSONField across all database backends**, including **SQLite, PostgreSQL, MySQL, and MariaDB**. This makes working with **semi-structured data** easier and more efficient, enabling:

- **Faster querying and filtering** on JSON data stored within relational databases.
- **Better compatibility with modern API development**, especially when integrating with **RESTful services and GraphQL**.

This feature is particularly valuable for developers building **data-heavy applications, APIs, and machine learning models** that require flexible data storage.

4. Security & Authentication Improvements

Django has always prioritized **security**, and version 5.1.x **enhances protection** against emerging web threats:

- **Stronger Password Hashing Algorithms** – The framework adopts **Argon2 and Bcrypt** as default hashing mechanisms, improving password security.
- **Improved CSRF Protection** – CSRF tokens are now **better encrypted**, preventing potential tampering or replay attacks.
- **Built-in Two-Factor Authentication (2FA) Support** – While Django previously relied on third-party packages, Django 5.1.x **integrates 2FA features** for better authentication security.

With these updates, **financial applications, government portals, and high-security platforms** can now **leverage Django with even more confidence**.

5. Enhanced Admin Panel & Customization Options

Django's **built-in admin interface** is a powerful tool for managing application data. The latest version includes:

- **Dark Mode Support** – A long-requested feature, the admin panel now supports **light and dark themes**, improving accessibility.
- **Live Search Enhancements** – The search functionality within the admin panel is now **faster and more intuitive**, allowing users to filter large datasets with ease.
- **Drag-and-Drop UI Improvements** – Admin users can now reorder **inline models** without additional JavaScript modifications.

These changes make Django's admin panel more **user-friendly**, especially for businesses relying on **custom admin dashboards** for data management.

6. Performance Enhancements & Reduced Memory Usage

Django 5.1.x includes **internal optimizations** that significantly reduce memory consumption and **improve response times**. Notable improvements include:

- **Faster Middleware Processing** – Streamlined request/response cycles mean Django apps can **handle more concurrent users** efficiently.

7

- **Optimized Static Files Handling** – Reduces **unnecessary file operations**, improving page load speeds for sites with **large CSS/JavaScript assets**.

For developers building **high-performance applications**, these updates result in **noticeable speed gains**.

Comparing Django with Other Web Frameworks (Flask, FastAPI, Laravel, etc.)

When choosing a **web framework**, developers often compare Django with **other popular options**, such as **Flask, FastAPI, and Laravel**. Each framework has its **strengths and weaknesses**, making them suitable for different types of projects.

Let's break down how Django compares to these alternatives.

Django vs. Flask

Feature	Django	Flask
Type	Full-stack framework	Micro-framework
Ease of Use	Includes built-in features for rapid development	Requires third-party extensions for authentication, ORM, etc.
Scalability	Handles large-scale applications efficiently	Best suited for small-to-medium projects
Security	Built-in security mechanisms	Relies on external libraries for advanced security
Admin Panel	Built-in Django Admin	No built-in admin panel
Database ORM	Django ORM (Highly optimized)	SQLAlchemy (Powerful but separate)

Verdict: Use Django if you need a **full-featured, scalable application**. Choose Flask if you prefer **lightweight flexibility** and want to build **custom solutions** from scratch.

8

Django vs. FastAPI

Feature	Django	FastAPI
Type	Full-stack framework	Asynchronous API framework
Performance	Optimized for traditional request-response cycles	Much faster for API-heavy applications
Async Support	Partial (Improving with Django 5.1.x)	Fully asynchronous from the ground up
Use Case	Full web applications, content-heavy sites	High-performance APIs, real-time applications
Learning Curve	Beginner-friendly	Requires understanding of async programming

Verdict: Use Django for building **full-stack web applications** and **FastAPI** for **performance-intensive APIs** that rely on real-time processing.

Django vs. Laravel (PHP Framework)

Feature	Django	Laravel
Language	Python	PHP
Ease of Learning	Easier for Python developers	Easier for PHP developers
Performance	Faster due to Python's efficiency	Slightly slower, but optimized with PHP 8
ORM	Django ORM	Eloquent (Powerful, but more complex)
Security	Strong built-in protections	Secure but requires additional configuration

Verdict: If your team **prefers Python**, Django is the clear winner. If your team has **PHP expertise**, Laravel offers similar capabilities within the PHP ecosystem.

Django 5.1.x **solidifies Django as a top choice** for modern web development, providing:

1. **Better async support for high-performance applications.**
2. **Stronger ORM optimization for database-heavy workloads.**
3. **Security enhancements to protect against modern threats.**
4. **Performance improvements that make Django faster and more efficient.**

When compared to other frameworks, Django **remains the best option** for developers who want a **scalable, secure, and full-featured web framework** that balances **ease of use with powerful capabilities**.

Setting Up Your Development Environment

Before diving into Django development, it's essential to set up a **proper development environment**. A well-configured environment ensures **smooth workflow, better debugging, and project scalability**.

Installing Python and Virtual Environments

Step 1: Checking If Python is Installed

Django is built with **Python**, so the first step is to ensure Python is installed on your system.

Open a terminal (or command prompt) and run:

```sh
CopyEdit
python --version
```

or

```sh
CopyEdit
python3 --version
```

If Python is installed, you should see an output similar to:

```nginx
CopyEdit
Python 3.10.12
```

Django 5.1.x **requires Python 3.10 or higher**. If your Python version is lower, you'll need to upgrade.

Step 2: Installing Python

For Windows

1. Download the latest version of **Python** from the official site:
   https://www.python.org/downloads/
2. Run the installer and check the box **"Add Python to PATH"** before clicking Install.

3. Once installed, verify the installation:
sh
CopyEdit
```
python --version
```

For macOS

Mac users can install Python using **Homebrew**:

sh
CopyEdit
```
brew install python
```

Once installed, verify it:

sh
CopyEdit
```
python3 --version
```

For Linux (Ubuntu/Debian)

Most Linux distributions come with Python pre-installed. However, you can upgrade it using:

sh
CopyEdit
```
sudo apt update
sudo apt install python3
```

To check the installation:

sh
CopyEdit
```
python3 --version
```

Step 3: Setting Up a Virtual Environment

A **virtual environment** is used to isolate Python dependencies **for each project**, preventing conflicts between different packages.

To create a virtual environment, follow these steps:

Step 3.1: Install venv (if not already installed)

Most Python distributions include venv. If not, install it using:

For Windows/macOS/Linux:

sh
CopyEdit
```
python3 -m pip install --upgrade pip
```

Step 3.2: Create a Virtual Environment

Navigate to your project directory and create a virtual environment:

```sh
CopyEdit
python3 -m venv my_django_env
```

This will create a folder named my_django_env, which will store dependencies.

Step 3.3: Activate the Virtual Environment

For Windows:

```sh
CopyEdit
my_django_env\Scripts\activate
```

For macOS/Linux:

```sh
CopyEdit
source my_django_env/bin/activate
```

Once activated, the terminal will display (my_django_env), indicating that the environment is active.

To deactivate the environment later, run:

```sh
CopyEdit
deactivate
```

Installing Django 5.1.x

Once the virtual environment is activated, install Django using **pip** (Python's package manager).

13

Run:

sh
CopyEdit
```
pip install django==5.1
```

To verify that Django installed correctly, check the version:

sh
CopyEdit
```
python -m django --version
```

The output should display:

CopyEdit
```
5.1
```

Django is now installed and ready to use!

Creating Your First Django Project

Now that Django is installed, let's create a **new Django project**.

Step 1: Create a Django Project

Navigate to your working directory where you want to store your project files and run:

sh
CopyEdit
```
django-admin startproject myproject
```

This creates a folder named myproject with the following structure:

lua
CopyEdit
```
myproject/
```

```
| -- manage.py
| -- myproject/
|   | -- __init__.py
|   | -- settings.py
|   | -- urls.py
|   | -- asgi.py
|   | -- wsgi.py
```

Here's what each file does:

- manage.py – A command-line tool for managing the project (running migrations, starting the server, etc.).
- settings.py – Contains project configurations (database, middleware, static files, etc.).
- urls.py – Manages URL routing for the application.
- asgi.py / wsgi.py – Entry points for **ASGI/Wsgi servers**, allowing deployment.

Step 2: Running the Development Server

Navigate into your project folder:

sh
CopyEdit
cd myproject

Start the development server with:

sh
CopyEdit
python manage.py runserver

If everything is set up correctly, you will see an output like:

csharp
CopyEdit
Watching for file changes with StatReloader

15

Performing system checks...

Django version 5.1, using settings 'myproject.settings'
Starting development server at http://127.0.0.1:8000/
Quit the server with CONTROL-C.

Open your browser and go to http://127.0.0.1:8000/.

You should see Django's **default welcome page**, confirming that your project is working!

Step 3: Creating a Django App

A **Django project** consists of multiple **apps**. Each app is a **modular component** that handles a specific function (e.g., user authentication, blog, API).

To create a new app, run:

sh
CopyEdit
```
python manage.py startapp blog
```

This creates a folder named blog/ with the following structure:

lua
CopyEdit
```
blog/
|-- migrations/
|-- __init__.py
|-- admin.py
|-- apps.py
|-- models.py
|-- tests.py
|-- views.py
```

16

Each file serves a purpose:

- models.py – Defines database models.
- views.py – Handles logic and data processing.
- admin.py – Manages the Django Admin Panel.
- tests.py – Contains test cases for the app.

Step 4: Registering the App in settings.py

Before using the new app, **register it in Django's settings**.

Open myproject/settings.py and add 'blog' under **INSTALLED_APPS**:

```python
CopyEdit
INSTALLED_APPS = [
    'django.contrib.admin',
    'django.contrib.auth',
    'django.contrib.contenttypes',
    'django.contrib.sessions',
    'django.contrib.messages',
    'django.contrib.staticfiles',
    'blog',  # New app added here
]
```

This tells Django to recognize the blog app when running the server.

Step 5: Defining a Simple View

To test the new app, open blog/views.py and create a simple function:

```python
CopyEdit
from django.http import HttpResponse

def home(request):
```

17

```
    return HttpResponse("Hello, Django 5.1.x!")
```

Then, open blog/urls.py (create it if missing) and define a **URL route**:

python
CopyEdit
```python
from django.urls import path
from .views import home

urlpatterns = [
    path('', home, name='home'),
]
```

Next, link the blog/urls.py to the main urls.py. Open myproject/urls.py and modify it:

python
CopyEdit
```python
from django.contrib import admin
from django.urls import path, include

urlpatterns = [
    path('admin/', admin.site.urls),
    path('', include('blog.urls')),  # Include blog app routes
]
```

Step 6: Testing the App

Restart the Django server:

sh
CopyEdit
```sh
python manage.py runserver
```

Now, visit http://127.0.0.1:8000/ in your browser.

You should see **"Hello, Django 5.1.x!"** displayed.

18

This confirms that your **Django project and app are working correctly!** 🎉

Chapter 2: Understanding Django's Core Architecture

Django follows a well-structured architecture that separates concerns efficiently, making web development **organized, scalable, and maintainable**. At the heart of Django's design is the **MTV (Model-Template-View) pattern**, which dictates how different components of a Django application interact.

The MTV (Model-Template-View) Pattern

Django follows the **MTV (Model-Template-View)** architecture, which is conceptually similar to the **MVC (Model-View-Controller)** pattern used in other frameworks. The MTV structure ensures **separation of concerns**, allowing developers to organize code into independent but interconnected components.

1. What is MTV?

In Django's **MTV pattern**:

- **Model (M)** – Manages database operations and defines the data structure.
- **Template (T)** – Handles the user interface (UI) and presentation layer.
- **View (V)** – Contains business logic and controls the flow of data between models and templates.

2. How MTV Works in Django

When a user interacts with a Django web application, the MTV flow looks like this:

1. **User makes a request** → Django's urls.py directs it to the appropriate view.
2. **View processes the request** → Fetches or updates data from the model.
3. **Model interacts with the database** → Queries data and returns it to the view.
4. **View passes data to the template** → The template dynamically generates an HTML response.
5. **User sees the final web page** → The response is sent back to the browser.

This approach **keeps business logic, database interaction, and presentation separate**, making Django applications **modular and easier to maintain**.

Django Project Structure Overview

When you create a new Django project, it generates a **standard directory structure** to organize code effectively.

Let's examine the key files in a Django project:

```
lua
CopyEdit
myproject/
|-- manage.py
|-- myproject/
|   |-- __init__.py
|   |-- settings.py
|   |-- urls.py
|   |-- asgi.py
|   |-- wsgi.py
|-- myapp/
|   |-- __init__.py
|   |-- admin.py
|   |-- apps.py
|   |-- models.py
|   |-- views.py
|   |-- urls.py
|   |-- templates/
|   |-- static/
```

Each file has a **specific role** in Django's architecture. Let's go through them one by one.

1. settings.py – Project Configuration File

The settings.py **file** contains all configurations for your Django project, such as **database settings, middleware, installed apps, static files, security settings**, and more.

Key Sections in settings.py

a) Installed Applications

The INSTALLED_APPS section defines all the apps used in the Django project:

```python
CopyEdit
INSTALLED_APPS = [
    'django.contrib.admin',
    'django.contrib.auth',
    'django.contrib.contenttypes',
    'django.contrib.sessions',
    'django.contrib.messages',
    'django.contrib.staticfiles',
    'myapp',  # Custom application
]
```

Any app you create must be added here to be recognized by Django.

b) Middleware Configuration

Django uses middleware to process requests before they reach the view:

```python
CopyEdit
MIDDLEWARE = [
    'django.middleware.security.SecurityMiddleware',
    'django.contrib.sessions.middleware.SessionMiddleware',
    'django.middleware.common.CommonMiddleware',
    'django.middleware.csrf.CsrfViewMiddleware',
    'django.middleware.auth.AuthenticationMiddleware',
    'django.middleware.clickjacking.XFrameOptionsMiddleware',
]
```

Middleware provides features like **security enforcement, session management, and authentication handling**.

c) Database Configuration

Django supports multiple databases. The default configuration uses **SQLite**, but you can switch to **PostgreSQL, MySQL, or other databases**:

```python
CopyEdit
DATABASES = {
    'default': {
        'ENGINE': 'django.db.backends.postgresql',
        'NAME': 'mydatabase',
        'USER': 'myuser',
        'PASSWORD': 'mypassword',
        'HOST': 'localhost',
        'PORT': '5432',
    }
}
```

d) Static and Media Files

Django separates **static files (CSS, JS, images)** and **media uploads**:

```python
CopyEdit
STATIC_URL = '/static/'
MEDIA_URL = '/media/'

STATICFILES_DIRS = [BASE_DIR / "static"]
MEDIA_ROOT = BASE_DIR / "media"
```

These settings are crucial when dealing with **front-end assets and user uploads**.

2. urls.py – URL Routing File

Django handles URL requests using **URL routing**. The urls.py file maps **URL patterns to views**, directing user requests to the right part of the application.

A basic urls.py file looks like this:

python
CopyEdit
```
from django.contrib import admin
from django.urls import path, include

urlpatterns = [
    path('admin/', admin.site.urls),
    path('', include('myapp.urls')),  # Redirect root URL to myapp
]
```

For individual apps, a separate urls.py is created:

python
CopyEdit
```
from django.urls import path
from . import views

urlpatterns = [
    path('', views.home, name='home'),
]
```

This ensures a **clean and modular URL structure**.

3. views.py – **Application Logic (Controller)**

The **views** in Django control how the application responds to requests. They retrieve data from models and pass it to templates.

A simple **view function**:

python
CopyEdit
```
from django.shortcuts import render

def home(request):
    return render(request, 'home.html', {'message': 'Welcome to Django!'})
```

This function:

1. Accepts a **request**.
2. Loads the **home.html** template.
3. Passes data (message) to the template for rendering.

For more complex applications, Django also supports **Class-Based Views (CBVs)**.

4. models.py – Defining the Database Schema

Django's **models** define the structure of the database. They use the **ORM (Object-Relational Mapper)** to simplify database operations.

A simple **model definition**:

python
CopyEdit
```
from django.db import models

class BlogPost(models.Model):
    title = models.CharField(max_length=255)
    content = models.TextField()
    published_date = models.DateTimeField(auto_now_add=True)

    def __str__(self):
        return self.title
```

To apply this model to the database, run:

sh
CopyEdit
```
python manage.py makemigrations
python manage.py migrate
```

This **automatically creates** the database tables based on the model definition.

5. admin.py – Django Admin Panel Configuration

Django provides a **built-in admin interface** for managing data. The admin.py file registers models for easy management.

To register the BlogPost model in Django Admin:

python
CopyEdit
```
from django.contrib import admin
from .models import BlogPost

admin.site.register(BlogPost)
```

After registering, you can **log in to the Django Admin panel** and manage BlogPost records **without writing SQL queries**.

To access the admin panel, start the Django server:

sh
CopyEdit
```
python manage.py runserver
```

Then, visit http://127.0.0.1:8000/admin/ and log in using the **superuser credentials**.

To create a superuser:

sh
CopyEdit
```
python manage.py createsuperuser
```

Follow the prompts to set up an admin account.

Django's App-Based Architecture (Reusability)

Django applications are **self-contained modules** that handle specific functionality within a project. This modular design allows:

- **Reusability** – Apps can be used across multiple projects.
- **Scalability** – Teams can work on different apps independently.
- **Better Maintainability** – Code is easier to manage when split into separate apps.

1. How Django Organizes Projects into Apps

A **Django project** is a **collection of apps** working together. Each app typically handles a specific feature, such as:

- **User authentication** (accounts/)
- **Blog functionality** (blog/)
- **E-commerce checkout** (checkout/)

A Django project can have **multiple apps**, and an app can be used in **multiple projects**.

Managing Django Apps

Every Django app has a predefined structure. To create a new app, follow these steps.

1. Creating an App in a Django Project

Navigate to your Django project directory and run:

sh

CopyEdit

```
python manage.py startapp blog
```

This creates a new folder named blog/ with the following structure:

lua

CopyEdit

```
blog/
|-- migrations/
|-- __init__.py
|-- admin.py
|-- apps.py
|-- models.py
|-- tests.py
|-- views.py
```

Each file serves a purpose:

- admin.py – Registers models in the Django Admin panel.
- apps.py – Configures app settings.

- models.py – Defines database structures.
- tests.py – Contains test cases for the app.
- views.py – Handles request-response logic.
- migrations/ – Stores database migration files.

2. Installing an App in a Django Project

After creating an app, Django **doesn't recognize it automatically**. You need to **register it** in the INSTALLED_APPS section of settings.py.

Open myproject/settings.py and add 'blog':

python

CopyEdit

```
INSTALLED_APPS = [

    'django.contrib.admin',

    'django.contrib.auth',

    'django.contrib.contenttypes',

    'django.contrib.sessions',

    'django.contrib.messages',

    'django.contrib.staticfiles',

    'blog',  # Registering the blog app

]
```

This step ensures Django loads the app whenever the project runs.

3. Creating URLs for the App

Each app can have its own urls.py to keep URL configurations modular.

a) Create a urls.py File for the App

Inside the blog/ directory, create urls.py (if it doesn't exist):

python

CopyEdit

```
from django.urls import path

from . import views


urlpatterns = [

    path('', views.home, name='home'),

]
```

b) Link the App's URLs to the Main Project

Next, open the **main project urls.py file** (myproject/urls.py) and include the app's URLs:

python

CopyEdit

```
from django.contrib import admin

from django.urls import path, include


urlpatterns = [

    path('admin/', admin.site.urls),
```

30

```
    path('blog/', include('blog.urls')),  # Linking the blog app

]
```

Now, visiting http://127.0.0.1:8000/blog/ will execute the home view from blog/views.py.

4. Creating a Simple View in the App

Open blog/views.py and define a function-based view:

python

CopyEdit

```
from django.http import HttpResponse


def home(request):
    return HttpResponse("Welcome to the Blog App!")
```

Restart the Django development server:

sh

CopyEdit

```
python manage.py runserver
```

Now, visiting http://127.0.0.1:8000/blog/ should display **"Welcome to the Blog App!"**.

31

Project-Level vs. App-Level Configuration

Django projects require **both global (project-level) and app-specific (app-level) configurations**. Understanding the difference between these is crucial for managing large-scale applications.

1. Project-Level Configuration

Project-level settings are stored in settings.py and affect the **entire Django project**.

Examples of Project-Level Settings:

- **Database Configuration**

python

CopyEdit

```python
DATABASES = {
    'default': {
        'ENGINE': 'django.db.backends.postgresql',
        'NAME': 'mydatabase',
        'USER': 'myuser',
        'PASSWORD': 'mypassword',
        'HOST': 'localhost',
        'PORT': '5432',
    }
}
```

- **Installed Applications**

python

CopyEdit

```
INSTALLED_APPS = [

    'django.contrib.admin',

    'django.contrib.auth',

    'blog',  # Global registration of an app

]
```

- **Static and Media Files**

python

CopyEdit

```
STATIC_URL = '/static/'

MEDIA_URL = '/media/'
```

These settings apply **across all apps** in the project.

2. App-Level Configuration

Each Django app has **local configurations** that apply **only to that specific app**. These are defined in apps.py.

Example: blog/apps.py

python

CopyEdit

```
from django.apps import AppConfig
```

```
class BlogConfig(AppConfig):

    default_auto_field = 'django.db.models.BigAutoField'

    name = 'blog'
```

App-level configurations are used when:

- Overriding default Django behavior for an app.
- Adding app-specific settings that shouldn't affect other parts of the project.

3. Overriding Project-Level Settings at the App Level

Sometimes, an app needs **custom configurations** that override global settings.

Example: **Custom Database for an App**
If an app needs a **separate database,** you can configure it in settings.py like this:

python

CopyEdit

```
DATABASES = {

    'default': {

        'ENGINE': 'django.db.backends.postgresql',

        'NAME': 'mydatabase',

        'USER': 'myuser',

    },

    'blog_db': {

        'ENGINE': 'django.db.backends.sqlite3',
```

```
        'NAME': 'blog.sqlite3',

    }

}
```

Then, in blog/models.py, direct the app to use the new database:

python

CopyEdit

```
class BlogPost(models.Model):

    title = models.CharField(max_length=255)

    content = models.TextField()


    class Meta:

        db_table = 'blog_post'

        app_label = 'blog'

        using = 'blog_db'  # Use the separate database
```

This ensures **only the blog app** uses the blog_db database.

Chapter 3: Working with Django Models and the ORM

Django's **Object-Relational Mapper (ORM)** provides a powerful way to interact with databases using Python code instead of raw SQL. The ORM allows developers to define **database schemas, manage relationships, perform queries, and update records** efficiently, without writing complex SQL statements.

What Are Models? Defining Database Schemas

A **model** in Django is a **Python class that defines the structure of a database table**. Each model maps to a table in the database, where each **class attribute** corresponds to a **column in the table**.

Django's ORM translates these models into SQL commands, allowing developers to perform database operations **without writing SQL manually**.

1. Creating a Basic Model in Django

Let's create a simple model for a **blog application**, where we store blog posts in the database.

Open models.py inside your Django app (blog/models.py) and define the BlogPost model:

python
CopyEdit
```python
from django.db import models

class BlogPost(models.Model):
    title = models.CharField(max_length=255)  # Title of the blog post
    content = models.TextField()  # Main blog content
    author = models.CharField(max_length=100)  # Name of the author
    published_date = models.DateTimeField(auto_now_add=True)  # Auto-set on creation

    def __str__(self):
        return self.title  # Return the title as the string representation
```

2. Understanding How Django Translates Models into Tables

The above model will be converted into a database table **blog_blogpost** (by default, Django names tables as appname_modelname).

Internally, Django converts the model into this SQL structure:

sql
CopyEdit

```sql
CREATE TABLE blog_blogpost (
    id SERIAL PRIMARY KEY,
    title VARCHAR(255) NOT NULL,
    content TEXT NOT NULL,
    author VARCHAR(100) NOT NULL,
    published_date TIMESTAMP DEFAULT CURRENT_TIMESTAMP
);
```

Django **automatically** creates an id field as the **primary key**, unless explicitly specified otherwise.

3. Model Metadata and Options

Django allows customization of models through **Meta options**, which define **how the model behaves** in the database.

For example, if we want to **change the default table name and ordering**:

python
CopyEdit

```python
class BlogPost(models.Model):
    title = models.CharField(max_length=255)
    content = models.TextField()
    author = models.CharField(max_length=100)
    published_date = models.DateTimeField(auto_now_add=True)

    class Meta:
        db_table = "blog_posts"  # Custom table name
        ordering = ["-published_date"]  # Order by newest first
```

37

This ensures our database table is named blog_posts instead of blog_blogpost and **orders posts by latest published date**.

Fields, Data Types, and Model Methods

1. Common Field Types in Django Models

Django provides various **field types** to store different kinds of data. Below are the most commonly used fields:

Field Type	Description
CharField(max_length=255)	Stores short text (e.g., names, titles).
TextField()	Stores long-form text (e.g., blog content, descriptions).
IntegerField()	Stores whole numbers.
FloatField()	Stores decimal numbers.
BooleanField()	Stores True or False values.
DateTimeField(auto_now_add=True)	Stores date and time; auto-set on creation.
EmailField()	Validates and stores email addresses.
URLField()	Stores website URLs.
FileField(upload_to='uploads/')	Handles file uploads.
ForeignKey()	Establishes a relationship between two models.

Example:

python
CopyEdit
```
class Product(models.Model):
    name = models.CharField(max_length=100)
    price = models.FloatField()
    available = models.BooleanField(default=True)
```

2. Defining Relationships Between Models

Django allows defining **relationships** between tables using **ForeignKey, OneToOneField, and ManyToManyField**.

a) One-to-Many (ForeignKey)

Each blog post belongs to **one author**, but an author can have **multiple blog posts**:

python
CopyEdit
```python
class Author(models.Model):
    name = models.CharField(max_length=100)
    email = models.EmailField()

class BlogPost(models.Model):
    title = models.CharField(max_length=255)
    author = models.ForeignKey(Author, on_delete=models.CASCADE)  # Relationship
```

b) One-to-One (OneToOneField)

Each user can have **one profile**, and each profile belongs to **one user**:

python
CopyEdit
```python
class UserProfile(models.Model):
    user = models.OneToOneField('auth.User', on_delete=models.CASCADE)
    bio = models.TextField()
```

c) Many-to-Many (ManyToManyField)

A student can enroll in **multiple courses**, and a course can have **multiple students**:

python
CopyEdit
```python
class Student(models.Model):
    name = models.CharField(max_length=100)

class Course(models.Model):
```

39

```python
name = models.CharField(max_length=100)
students = models.ManyToManyField(Student)
```

3. Adding Methods to Models

Django models can contain custom methods to perform actions on data.

Example: **Adding a method to format published date**:

python
CopyEdit
```python
class BlogPost(models.Model):
    title = models.CharField(max_length=255)
    published_date = models.DateTimeField(auto_now_add=True)

    def formatted_date(self):
        return self.published_date.strftime('%B %d, %Y')
```

Usage:

python
CopyEdit
```python
post = BlogPost.objects.get(id=1)
print(post.formatted_date())  # Output: "March 15, 2025"
```

Running Migrations and Applying Changes to the Database

Once models are defined, Django requires **migrations** to create and update database tables.

1. Creating Migrations

Migrations act as **version control for database changes**. Whenever a new model is added or modified, migrations must be created.

To generate migrations for an app:

sh
CopyEdit
```
python manage.py makemigrations blog
```

This creates a migration file in blog/migrations/:

bash
CopyEdit
```
blog/migrations/0001_initial.py
```

This file contains the SQL equivalent of model definitions.

2. Applying Migrations

After generating migrations, apply them to the database:

sh
CopyEdit
```
python manage.py migrate
```

This executes the migration script and **creates the necessary tables**.

3. Checking Migration History

To see a list of applied migrations:

sh
CopyEdit
```
python manage.py showmigrations
```

Example output:

csharp
CopyEdit
```
blog
 [X] 0001_initial
```

41

A **checked box ([X])** means the migration has been applied.

4. Rolling Back Migrations

If a migration causes an issue, it can be **rolled back**:

```sh
CopyEdit
python manage.py migrate blog 0001_initial
```

This reverts the blog app's database schema to its initial state.

5. Making Schema Changes

When modifying a model (e.g., adding a new field), Django requires additional migrations.

Example: **Adding a new category field**:

```python
CopyEdit
class BlogPost(models.Model):
    title = models.CharField(max_length=255)
    category = models.CharField(max_length=100, default='General')
```

Run the migration commands again:

```sh
CopyEdit
python manage.py makemigrations
python manage.py migrate
```

Django **updates the database structure automatically**.

42

Querying Data with Django ORM

Django's **Object-Relational Mapper (ORM)** allows developers to interact with the database using Python instead of raw SQL queries. The ORM provides a high-level API for performing CRUD operations (Create, Read, Update, Delete) and filtering data efficiently.

CRUD Operations (Create, Read, Update, Delete)

Django ORM follows an intuitive and structured approach for **managing database records**. Below are the fundamental operations:

1. Creating Records (INSERT Operation)

To create a new record in the database, use the create() method or instantiate a model object and call save().

Using .create() Method (Recommended for Simplicity)

python

CopyEdit

```python
from blog.models import BlogPost


# Create and save a new blog post
post = BlogPost.objects.create(
    title="Understanding Django ORM",
    content="Django ORM provides an abstraction layer...",
    author="John Doe"
)
```

Using .save() Method (For More Control)

python

CopyEdit

```
post = BlogPost(
    title="Exploring Django QuerySet",
    content="QuerySet allows filtering, ordering, and retrieving data...",
    author="Jane Smith"
)
post.save()  # Save the record to the database
```

Both methods will generate an SQL INSERT statement internally:

sql

CopyEdit

```
INSERT INTO blog_blogpost (title, content, author)
VALUES ('Understanding Django ORM', 'Django ORM provides...', 'John Doe');
```

2. Reading Records (SELECT Operation)

Django ORM provides multiple ways to **retrieve data** from the database.

Retrieve All Records

python

CopyEdit

```
posts = BlogPost.objects.all()
```

Equivalent SQL:

sql

CopyEdit

```sql
SELECT * FROM blog_blogpost;
```

Retrieve a Single Record by ID

python

CopyEdit

```python
post = BlogPost.objects.get(id=1)
```

Equivalent SQL:

sql

CopyEdit

```sql
SELECT * FROM blog_blogpost WHERE id = 1;
```

If the object does not exist, get() raises a DoesNotExist exception.

Retrieve the First or Last Record

python

CopyEdit

```python
first_post = BlogPost.objects.first()

last_post = BlogPost.objects.last()
```

45

Retrieving Specific Fields (Efficiency Optimization)

Fetching only selected fields reduces **query overhead**:

python

CopyEdit

```
posts = BlogPost.objects.values('title', 'author')
```

Equivalent SQL:

sql

CopyEdit

```
SELECT title, author FROM blog_blogpost;
```

Ordering Results

To retrieve posts **ordered by published date (newest first)**:

python

CopyEdit

```
posts = BlogPost.objects.order_by('-published_date')
```

Equivalent SQL:

sql

CopyEdit

```
SELECT * FROM blog_blogpost ORDER BY published_date DESC;
```

3. Updating Records (UPDATE Operation)

To update a record, modify its fields and call .save(), or use .update() for bulk updates.

Updating a Single Record

python

CopyEdit

```
post = BlogPost.objects.get(id=1)

post.title = "Updated Django ORM Title"

post.save()
```

Equivalent SQL:

sql

CopyEdit

```
UPDATE blog_blogpost

SET title = 'Updated Django ORM Title'

WHERE id = 1;
```

Bulk Updating Multiple Records

python

CopyEdit

```
BlogPost.objects.filter(author="John Doe").update(author="Jonathan Doe")
```

Equivalent SQL:

sql

CopyEdit

```sql
UPDATE blog_blogpost
SET author = 'Jonathan Doe'
WHERE author = 'John Doe';
```

4. Deleting Records (DELETE Operation)

Django ORM allows deleting records using .delete().

Deleting a Single Record

python

CopyEdit

```python
post = BlogPost.objects.get(id=1)
post.delete()
```

Equivalent SQL:

sql

CopyEdit

```sql
DELETE FROM blog_blogpost WHERE id = 1;
```

48

Bulk Deleting Multiple Records

python

CopyEdit

```python
BlogPost.objects.filter(author="Jane Smith").delete()
```

Equivalent SQL:

sql

CopyEdit

```sql
DELETE FROM blog_blogpost WHERE author = 'Jane Smith';
```

QuerySet API and Filtering Data

Django ORM provides the **QuerySet API**, which allows efficient querying of the database.

1. Filtering Data (filter(), exclude(), get())

Using filter() to Retrieve Specific Records

python

CopyEdit

```python
posts = BlogPost.objects.filter(author="John Doe")
```

Equivalent SQL:

sql

CopyEdit

```sql
SELECT * FROM blog_blogpost WHERE author = 'John Doe';
```

49

Using exclude() to Omit Certain Records

python

CopyEdit

```python
posts = BlogPost.objects.exclude(author="John Doe")
```

Equivalent SQL:

sql

CopyEdit

```sql
SELECT * FROM blog_blogpost WHERE author != 'John Doe';
```

Using get() to Fetch a Unique Record

python

CopyEdit

```python
post = BlogPost.objects.get(id=5)
```

⚠ **Caution**: get() should only be used when querying a single record. If multiple records match, it raises a MultipleObjectsReturned exception.

2. Using Lookups for Advanced Filtering

Django provides various lookup filters for more refined searches.

a) Filtering by Case-Insensitive Match (iexact)

python

CopyEdit

```python
posts = BlogPost.objects.filter(author__iexact="john doe")
```

Equivalent SQL:

sql

CopyEdit

```sql
SELECT * FROM blog_blogpost WHERE LOWER(author) = 'john doe';
```

b) Filtering by Partial Match (icontains)

python

CopyEdit

```python
posts = BlogPost.objects.filter(title__icontains="django")
```

Equivalent SQL:

sql

CopyEdit

```sql
SELECT * FROM blog_blogpost WHERE title ILIKE '%django%';
```

51

c) Filtering by Date (gte, lte)

python

CopyEdit

```
from django.utils.timezone import now


posts = BlogPost.objects.filter(published_date__gte=now())
```

Equivalent SQL:

sql

CopyEdit

```
SELECT * FROM blog_blogpost WHERE published_date >=
CURRENT_TIMESTAMP;
```

d) Filtering by Multiple Conditions (Q Objects for OR Queries)

Django's Q object allows complex queries using **OR conditions**:

python

CopyEdit

```
from django.db.models import Q


posts = BlogPost.objects.filter(Q(title__icontains="django") | Q(author="John Doe"))
```

52

Equivalent SQL:

sql

CopyEdit

```sql
SELECT * FROM blog_blogpost WHERE title ILIKE '%django%' OR author = 'John Doe';
```

3. Aggregation and Counting Records

Django provides built-in aggregation functions for **sum, count, min, max, and average**.

Counting Records

python

CopyEdit

```python
total_posts = BlogPost.objects.count()
```

Equivalent SQL:

sql

CopyEdit

```sql
SELECT COUNT(*) FROM blog_blogpost;
```

Finding the Earliest or Latest Entry

python

CopyEdit

```python
oldest_post = BlogPost.objects.earliest('published_date')

latest_post = BlogPost.objects.latest('published_date')
```

53

Calculating Aggregate Values

python

CopyEdit

```
from django.db.models import Avg


average_posts_per_author = BlogPost.objects.aggregate(Avg('id'))
```

Equivalent SQL:

sql

CopyEdit

```
SELECT AVG(id) FROM blog_blogpost;
```

Django ORM makes **database interactions intuitive and efficient,** enabling developers to **focus on business logic instead of SQL queries.**

Managing Database Relationships in Django

Django's **Object-Relational Mapper (ORM)** provides a structured way to define relationships between models. These relationships help manage **data integrity and dependencies** efficiently. Django supports three primary types of relationships:

1. **One-to-One Relationship (OneToOneField)** – Each record in **Model A** is linked to exactly one record in **Model B**.
2. **One-to-Many Relationship (ForeignKey)** – A record in **Model A** can be related to **multiple records** in **Model B**.

3. **Many-to-Many Relationship** (ManyToManyField) – Multiple records in **Model A** can relate to multiple records in **Model B**.

These relationships are critical when designing a **relational database** that ensures **efficiency, flexibility, and maintainability**. Let's explore each relationship type with examples.

1. One-to-One Relationship (OneToOneField)

A **One-to-One** relationship means that each instance of **Model A** is associated with exactly **one** instance of **Model B**. This is commonly used for **user profiles, settings, or extended information**.

Example: User and Profile

Each User should have **one and only one** Profile. The Profile model extends User without modifying its structure.

python

CopyEdit

```
from django.db import models

from django.contrib.auth.models import User


class Profile(models.Model):

    user = models.OneToOneField(User, on_delete=models.CASCADE)  # One-to-One link

    bio = models.TextField(blank=True)

    profile_picture = models.ImageField(upload_to='profiles/', null=True, blank=True)


    def __str__(self):
```

```python
return f"Profile of {self.user.username}"
```

Breaking Down the Code:

- The OneToOneField **creates a one-to-one relationship** with Django's built-in User model.
- on_delete=models.CASCADE ensures that if a User is deleted, their associated Profile is also removed.
- profile_picture allows an optional image upload.

Querying One-to-One Relationships:

Creating a Profile for a User

python

CopyEdit

```python
user = User.objects.create(username="john_doe")

profile = Profile.objects.create(user=user, bio="Software Developer")
```

Accessing Related Objects

python

CopyEdit

```python
user_profile = user.profile  # Access profile from user

print(user_profile.bio)  # Output: Software Developer
```

python

CopyEdit

```python
profile_user = profile.user  # Access user from profile
```

56

```
print(profile_user.username)  # Output: john_doe
```

Use Cases for One-to-One Relationships:

■ **Extending User Information** (Profiles, settings, preferences)
■ **Linking Additional Metadata** (e.g., API keys, permissions)
■ **Creating Separate Tables for Optional Data**

2. One-to-Many Relationship (ForeignKey)

A **One-to-Many** relationship means that each instance of **Model A** can be related to **multiple instances** of **Model B**, but each instance of **Model B** relates to **only one instance of Model A**.

This is the most commonly used relationship in Django. Examples include:

- A **blog post** can have multiple **comments**.
- A **category** can contain multiple **products**.
- A **user** can create multiple **orders**.

Example: BlogPost and Comments

Each BlogPost can have **multiple Comments**, but each Comment belongs to **only one** BlogPost.

python

CopyEdit

```
class BlogPost(models.Model):

    title = models.CharField(max_length=255)

    content = models.TextField()

    published_date = models.DateTimeField(auto_now_add=True)
```

57

```python
def __str__(self):

    return self.title


class Comment(models.Model):

    blog_post = models.ForeignKey(BlogPost, on_delete=models.CASCADE)  # One-to-Many link

    author = models.CharField(max_length=100)

    text = models.TextField()

    created_at = models.DateTimeField(auto_now_add=True)


    def __str__(self):

        return f"Comment by {self.author} on {self.blog_post.title}"
```

Breaking Down the Code:

- ForeignKey(BlogPost, on_delete=models.CASCADE) defines a **one-to-many** relationship.
- on_delete=models.CASCADE means **if a BlogPost is deleted, all related Comments are also deleted**.
- Each comment **references a single BlogPost**, but a BlogPost can have **many comments**.

Querying One-to-Many Relationships:

Creating a Blog Post and Adding Comments

python

CopyEdit

```
post = BlogPost.objects.create(title="Django ORM", content="Understanding Django ORM")

comment1 = Comment.objects.create(blog_post=post, author="Alice", text="Great post!")

comment2 = Comment.objects.create(blog_post=post, author="Bob", text="Very informative!")
```

Retrieving Related Comments for a Blog Post

python

CopyEdit

```
comments = post.comment_set.all()  # Get all comments for a post

for comment in comments:

    print(comment.text)
```

Accessing the Blog Post from a Comment

python

CopyEdit

```
print(comment1.blog_post.title)  # Output: Django ORM
```

Use Cases for One-to-Many Relationships:

■ **Blog Posts and Comments**
■ **Categories and Products**
■ **Authors and Books**

3. Many-to-Many Relationship (ManyToManyField)

A **Many-to-Many** relationship means that **multiple instances of Model A** can be related to **multiple instances of Model B**.

Examples include:

- **Students and Courses** – A student can enroll in multiple courses, and a course can have multiple students.
- **Authors and Books** – A book can have multiple authors, and an author can write multiple books.
- **Tags and Blog Posts** – A blog post can have multiple tags, and a tag can belong to multiple blog posts.

Example: Students and Courses

Each Student can enroll in multiple Course objects, and each Course can have multiple Student objects.

python

CopyEdit

```python
class Student(models.Model):

    name = models.CharField(max_length=100)

    email = models.EmailField()


    def __str__(self):

        return self.name
```

60

```python
class Course(models.Model):
    title = models.CharField(max_length=255)
    students = models.ManyToManyField(Student)  # Many-to-Many link

    def __str__(self):
        return self.title
```

Querying Many-to-Many Relationships:

Adding Students to a Course

python

CopyEdit

```python
student1 = Student.objects.create(name="Alice", email="alice@example.com")
student2 = Student.objects.create(name="Bob", email="bob@example.com")

course = Course.objects.create(title="Django Web Development")
course.students.add(student1, student2)  # Adding multiple students
```

Retrieving Students Enrolled in a Course

python

CopyEdit

```python
students_in_course = course.students.all()
```

61

```
for student in students_in_course:

    print(student.name)
```

Finding Courses a Student is Enrolled In

python

CopyEdit

```
courses_of_student = student1.course_set.all()

for course in courses_of_student:

    print(course.title)
```

Use Cases for Many-to-Many Relationships:

■ **Students and Courses**
■ **Tags and Blog Posts**
■ **Authors and Books**

Using Django's Built-in Admin Panel for Model Management

Django comes with a powerful **built-in admin panel** that allows developers and administrators to **manage database records, create and update entries, and perform administrative tasks** without writing SQL queries. The admin panel is automatically generated based on Django models and provides a **user-friendly interface for managing application data**.

1. Enabling Django Admin

Django's admin panel is included by default in new projects. To ensure it is enabled, check that **django.contrib.admin** is listed in INSTALLED_APPS inside settings.py:

python

CopyEdit

```
INSTALLED_APPS = [

    'django.contrib.admin',  # Enables the admin panel

    'django.contrib.auth',

    'django.contrib.contenttypes',

    'django.contrib.sessions',

    'django.contrib.messages',

    'django.contrib.staticfiles',

]
```

Additionally, verify that **admin.site.urls** is included in the project's urls.py:

python

CopyEdit

```
from django.contrib import admin

from django.urls import path


urlpatterns = [

    path('admin/', admin.site.urls),  # Admin panel accessible at /admin/

]
```

63

Now, start the development server:

sh

CopyEdit

```
python manage.py runserver
```

Visit http://127.0.0.1:8000/admin/ in a web browser. Django will prompt for **superuser credentials**.

2. Creating a Superuser (Admin Account)

To log in to the Django admin panel, create a **superuser** account:

sh

CopyEdit

```
python manage.py createsuperuser
```

Follow the prompts to enter:

- **Username**
- **Email**
- **Password**

Once created, restart the server:

sh

CopyEdit

```
python manage.py runserver
```

64

Now, log in to http://127.0.0.1:8000/admin/ with the credentials provided.

3. Registering Models in the Admin Panel

By default, Django's admin panel **does not display models**. We need to **register models** in admin.py so they appear in the admin interface.

Example: Registering a Model in admin.py

Let's assume we have a BlogPost model:

python

CopyEdit

```python
from django.db import models


class BlogPost(models.Model):
    title = models.CharField(max_length=255)

    content = models.TextField()

    author = models.CharField(max_length=100)

    published_date = models.DateTimeField(auto_now_add=True)


    def __str__(self):
        return self.title
```

To make this model accessible in the admin panel, open admin.py and register it:

python

CopyEdit

```
from django.contrib import admin
from .models import BlogPost


admin.site.register(BlogPost)
```

Now, refresh http://127.0.0.1:8000/admin/ – the **BlogPost model** will appear in the panel.

4. Customizing the Admin Panel

Django allows extensive customization of the admin interface for a better user experience.

4.1 Customizing the Model Display

To customize how models appear in the admin panel, use the Admin class:

python

CopyEdit

```
class BlogPostAdmin(admin.ModelAdmin):
    list_display = ('title', 'author', 'published_date')  # Display these fields in the list
    search_fields = ('title', 'author')  # Enable search by title and author
    list_filter = ('published_date',)  # Add filter sidebar by date
```

66

admin.site.register(BlogPost, BlogPostAdmin)

This enhances the **model listing page**:

- **List Display** (list_display) – Shows specific columns in the admin interface.
- **Search Fields** (search_fields) – Adds a search bar for specific fields.
- **List Filter** (list_filter) – Adds filtering options for easy record management.

4.2 Enabling Inline Editing (Related Models Management)

If a model has a **One-to-Many** or **Many-to-Many** relationship, Django allows managing related records **within the parent model's admin page**.

Example: BlogPost and Comments

Assume a **Comment** model linked to BlogPost:

python

CopyEdit

```
class Comment(models.Model):

    blog_post = models.ForeignKey(BlogPost, on_delete=models.CASCADE)

    author = models.CharField(max_length=100)

    text = models.TextField()

    created_at = models.DateTimeField(auto_now_add=True)


    def __str__(self):

        return f"Comment by {self.author}"
```

To manage **comments inside the BlogPost admin panel**, use TabularInline:

python

CopyEdit

```
class CommentInline(admin.TabularInline):

    model = Comment

    extra = 1  # Allows adding a new comment directly from BlogPost admin


class BlogPostAdmin(admin.ModelAdmin):

    list_display = ('title', 'author', 'published_date')

    inlines = [CommentInline]  # Display comments inside blog post admin


admin.site.register(BlogPost, BlogPostAdmin)

admin.site.register(Comment)  # Comments still appear separately in admin
```

Now, when editing a blog post in the admin panel, **comments can be added or edited directly inside the post's page**.

5. Managing Users and Permissions

Django allows managing **users, groups, and permissions** via the admin panel.

5.1 Creating User Groups and Permissions

- Navigate to **/admin/** → **Users** → **Add a user**
- Assign **staff status** to allow admin access.
- Navigate to **/admin/** → **Groups** → **Add Group** to create user roles.

68

5.2 Assigning Permissions to Groups

Example: Create an **"Editors"** group that can modify blog posts but cannot delete them.

1. Go to **Admin Panel → Groups → Add Group**
2. Select **"Editors"** and assign permissions like:
   - ■ Can change blog post
   - ✕ Cannot delete blog post
3. Add users to the "Editors" group.

Users in this group can edit blog posts **but cannot delete them**.

6. Advanced Features: Search, Filtering, and Actions

Django's admin panel supports additional features for **enhanced usability**.

6.1 Adding Advanced Search

To enable searching across multiple fields:

python

CopyEdit

```
class BlogPostAdmin(admin.ModelAdmin):
    search_fields = ('title', 'content', 'author')  # Searchable fields
```

Now, the admin panel will include a **search bar** to find posts **by title, content, or author**.

6.2 Filtering Data

The **list filter** option adds a **sidebar** with filter options.

python

CopyEdit

```
class BlogPostAdmin(admin.ModelAdmin):
    list_filter = ('author', 'published_date')
```

Now, admins can filter blog posts **by author and published date**.

6.3 Bulk Actions

Django allows **bulk actions** to be performed on multiple records.

Example: Adding a bulk action to **publish multiple blog posts**:

python

CopyEdit

```
class BlogPostAdmin(admin.ModelAdmin):
    actions = ['publish_posts']


    def publish_posts(self, request, queryset):
        queryset.update(published_date=timezone.now())  # Bulk update publish date
        self.message_user(request, "Selected posts have been published.")


    publish_posts.short_description = "Publish selected posts"
```

Admins can now select multiple posts and **publish them in one click**.

Chapter 4: Views, URL Routing, and Django Templates

Django's **view system** acts as the **controller** in the Model-Template-View (MTV) pattern, handling user requests and returning responses. Views are responsible for **processing data, interacting with models, and rendering templates** to provide a dynamic web experience.

Django provides two main approaches for writing views:

1. **Function-Based Views (FBVs)** – Simple, procedural-style views.
2. **Class-Based Views (CBVs)** – More structured, reusable, and scalable views.

Handling Requests with Function-Based Views (FBVs)

A **Function-Based View (FBV)** is a Python function that takes a **request** and returns a **response**. It follows a straightforward approach, making it easy to read and understand.

1. Basic Structure of an FBV

Each Django view must accept a request object as the first argument and return an HttpResponse object.

Example: **A simple view returning plain text**

```python
CopyEdit
from django.http import HttpResponse

def home(request):
    return HttpResponse("Welcome to Django!")
```

- The function takes request as an argument.
- HttpResponse sends back text content to the browser.

To access this view, map it to a URL in urls.py:

python
CopyEdit
```python
from django.urls import path
from . import views

urlpatterns = [
    path('', views.home, name='home'),
]
```

Now, visiting http://127.0.0.1:8000/ will display **"Welcome to Django!"**.

2. Rendering Templates in FBVs

Instead of returning plain text, Django views **render HTML templates** using the render() function.

Example: **Rendering a template using FBV**

python
CopyEdit
```python
from django.shortcuts import render

def home(request):
    return render(request, 'home.html')
```

Django will look for home.html inside a templates/ directory:

lua
CopyEdit
```
myapp/
│-- templates/
│   │-- home.html
```

Example **home.html** file:

html
CopyEdit
```html
<!DOCTYPE html>
<html>
<head>
    <title>Home Page</title>
</head>
<body>
    <h1>Welcome to Django!</h1>
</body>
</html>
```

3. Passing Data to Templates

Django allows passing **context data** to templates.

Example: **Rendering a template with dynamic data**

python
CopyEdit
```python
def home(request):
    context = {'title': 'Welcome to Django', 'message': 'This is a dynamic message!'}
    return render(request, 'home.html', context)
```

Modify home.html to display the data:

html
CopyEdit
```html
<h1>{{ title }}</h1>
<p>{{ message }}</p>
```

Now, visiting http://127.0.0.1:8000/ will show:

csharp
CopyEdit
Welcome to Django
This is a dynamic message!

4. Handling URL Parameters in FBVs

Django allows capturing **URL parameters** and passing them to views.

Example: Retrieving a blog post by ID

Define the view:

python
CopyEdit
```python
def blog_post(request, post_id):
    return HttpResponse(f"Displaying Blog Post {post_id}")
```

Map it in urls.py:

python
CopyEdit
```python
urlpatterns = [
    path('post/<int:post_id>/', views.blog_post, name='blog_post'),
]
```

Visiting http://127.0.0.1:8000/post/10/ will return:

nginx
CopyEdit
Displaying Blog Post 10

5. Handling HTTP Methods in FBVs

Django views can handle **GET and POST requests** using conditionals.

Example: **Handling different HTTP methods in a view**

```python
CopyEdit
from django.http import JsonResponse

def contact_form(request):
    if request.method == "GET":
        return JsonResponse({"message": "Display contact form"})
    elif request.method == "POST":
        return JsonResponse({"message": "Form submitted successfully"})
```

- If accessed via **GET**, it returns a message to display the form.
- If accessed via **POST**, it processes the form submission.

Using Class-Based Views (CBVs) for Cleaner Code

Django provides **Class-Based Views (CBVs)** as an alternative to FBVs. CBVs **promote reusability and cleaner code** by leveraging **object-oriented programming (OOP) principles**.

1. Why Use Class-Based Views?

- **More structured and reusable** – Avoids repetitive code.
- **Built-in generic views** – Provides common views like ListView, DetailView, etc.
- **Cleaner handling of HTTP methods** – No need for if request.method == "GET".

2. Basic Class-Based View Example

A **CBV** is defined by **inheriting from Django's built-in view classes**.

Example: **A simple class-based view returning an HTTP response**

python
CopyEdit
```
from django.http import HttpResponse
from django.views import View

class HomeView(View):
    def get(self, request):
        return HttpResponse("Welcome to Django - Class-Based View!")
```

Map it in urls.py:

python
CopyEdit
```
urlpatterns = [
    path('', HomeView.as_view(), name='home'),
]
```

CBVs require calling .as_view() to function correctly.

3. Rendering Templates in CBVs

CBVs **separate logic** into distinct methods for better readability.

Example: **Rendering a template using** TemplateView

python
CopyEdit
```
from django.views.generic import TemplateView

class HomeView(TemplateView):
    template_name = "home.html"
```

Since TemplateView is a **generic view**, it automatically renders home.html without needing an explicit render() function.

76

4. Passing Context Data in CBVs

Use get_context_data() to pass data to templates.

Example:

```python
CopyEdit
class HomeView(TemplateView):
    template_name = "home.html"

    def get_context_data(self, **kwargs):
        context = super().get_context_data(**kwargs)
        context['title'] = "Django Class-Based Views"
        return context
```

Modify home.html:

```html
CopyEdit
<h1>{{ title }}</h1>
```

Visiting http://127.0.0.1:8000/ will display:

```vbnet
CopyEdit
Django Class-Based Views
```

5. Handling URL Parameters in CBVs

CBVs can retrieve URL parameters using self.kwargs.

Example: **Retrieving a blog post by ID**

```python
CopyEdit
from django.views.generic import DetailView
from .models import BlogPost
```

77

```
class BlogPostView(DetailView):
    model = BlogPost
    template_name = "blog_post.html"
    context_object_name = "post"
```

Map it in urls.py:

python
CopyEdit
```
urlpatterns = [
    path('post/<int:pk>/', BlogPostView.as_view(), name='blog_post'),
]
```

Now, visiting http://127.0.0.1:8000/post/1/ retrieves **BlogPost with ID=1**.

6. Using Django's Built-in Generic Views

Django provides **generic views** that **eliminate repetitive code**:

Generic View	Use Case
ListView	Displays a list of objects.
DetailView	Displays a single object's details.
CreateView	Handles form submissions for new records.
UpdateView	Handles form submissions for editing records.
DeleteView	Handles record deletion.

Example: Displaying a List of Blog Posts using ListView

python
CopyEdit
```
from django.views.generic import ListView
from .models import BlogPost

class BlogPostListView(ListView):
```

78

```
model = BlogPost
template_name = "blog_list.html"
context_object_name = "posts"
```

Django automatically:

- Fetches all BlogPost objects.
- Renders them in blog_list.html.

Django views allow developers to **build scalable applications with minimal code repetition**

URL Routing and Django Template Language (DTL)

Django's URL routing system allows developers to map incoming HTTP requests to specific views, ensuring a structured and navigable web application. Additionally, the Django Template Language (DTL) provides a powerful way to generate dynamic HTML pages using data from views.

URL Routing and Path Converters

Django follows a URL-driven architecture, meaning every request is mapped to a view function or class-based view. The routing is defined in the urls.py file of the project or an app.

1. Defining Basic URL Patterns

A Django project's main urls.py is located inside the project folder and typically looks like this:

python

CopyEdit

from django.contrib import admin

from django.urls import path

```
from myapp import views


urlpatterns = [

    path('admin/', admin.site.urls),  # Django Admin URL

    path('', views.home, name='home'),  # Homepage

]
```

2. Using Path Converters for Dynamic URLs

Path converters allow capturing dynamic values from URLs and passing them to views.

Path Converter	Meaning	Example URL	Example View Parameter
`int:`	Integer	`/post/10/`	`post_id=10`
`str:`	String (no slashes)	`/user/john/`	`username='john'`
`slug:`	Slug (letters, numbers, hyphens)	`/blog/my-first-post/`	`slug='my-first-post'`
`uuid:`	UUID format	`/product/550e8400-e29b-41d4-a716-446655440000/`	`uuid='550e8400-e29b-41d4-a716-446655440000'`
`path:`	Captures the full path (including slashes)	`/media/uploads/file.pdf`	`filepath='uploads/file.pdf'`

Example: Dynamic Blog Post URL

In urls.py:

python

CopyEdit

urlpatterns = [

80

```python
    path('post/<int:post_id>/', views.blog_post, name='blog_post'),
]
```

In views.py:

python

CopyEdit

```python
from django.http import HttpResponse


def blog_post(request, post_id):
    return HttpResponse(f"Displaying Blog Post {post_id}")
```

Now, visiting http://127.0.0.1:8000/post/5/ **will display:**

nginx

CopyEdit

Displaying Blog Post 5

3. Using re_path() **for Regular Expressions**

For more complex patterns, re_path() **allows regular expressions in URL routing.**

python

CopyEdit

```python
from django.urls import re_path


urlpatterns = [
```

```
    re_path(r'^post/(?P<post_id>\d{4})/$', views.blog_post, name='blog_post'),
```
]

This route only matches four-digit post_id **values (e.g.,** /post/2023/**).**

4. Including App-Level URLs for Modular Routing

Instead of defining all URLs in the project's urls.py**, Django allows including app-level URLs.**

In the project's urls.py**:**

python

CopyEdit

```python
from django.urls import path, include


urlpatterns = [
    path('admin/', admin.site.urls),
    path('blog/', include('blog.urls')),  # Include blog app URLs
]
```


Then, create blog/urls.py**:**

python

CopyEdit

```python
from django.urls import path
from . import views
```

82

```
urlpatterns = [

    path('', views.blog_home, name='blog_home'),  # Default blog page

    path('<int:post_id>/', views.blog_post, name='blog_post'),

]
```

Now, visiting http://127.0.0.1:8000/blog/5/ **will correctly route to the blog post.**

Working with Django Template Language (DTL)

Django's Template System allows separating logic from presentation, enabling dynamic content rendering in HTML.

Templates are stored inside an app's templates/ **directory:**

lua

CopyEdit

```
myapp/

 | -- templates/

 |    | -- home.html

 |    | -- blog/

 |    |    | -- post_detail.html
```

1. Rendering a Template from a View

A Django view can pass data to a template using render():

python

CopyEdit

```python
from django.shortcuts import render


def home(request):
    context = {'title': 'Welcome to Django Templates'}
    return render(request, 'home.html', context)
```

2. Using Template Variables

Inside home.html, **use** {{ }} **to display dynamic data:**

html

CopyEdit

```html
<h1>{{ title }}</h1>
```

When the page loads, it will display:

css

CopyEdit

```
Welcome to Django Templates
```

3. Using Control Structures in Templates

DTL supports if statements, loops, and filters for dynamic content.

a) Using {% if %} Statements

html

CopyEdit

```
{% if user.is_authenticated %}
    <p>Welcome, {{ user.username }}!</p>
{% else %}
    <p>Please log in.</p>
{% endif %}
```

b) Using {% for %} Loops

html

CopyEdit

```
<ul>
    {% for post in posts %}
        <li>{{ post.title }} by {{ post.author }}</li>
    {% endfor %}
</ul>
```

c) Using Template Filters

Template filters modify data before displaying it.

html

CopyEdit

```html
<p>{{ content|truncatewords:20 }}</p>  <!-- Limits content to 20 words -->
<p>{{ published_date|date:"F d, Y" }}</p>  <!-- Formats date -->
```

Common Filters:

- length – **Returns the number of items in a list.**
- lower / upper – **Converts text to lowercase or uppercase.**
- default:"text" – **Provides a default value if the variable is empty.**
- slice:"5" – **Limits a list to the first 5 items.**

4. Template Inheritance for Reusability

Django supports template inheritance, which reduces repetition in HTML files.

a) Creating a Base Template (base.html)

html

CopyEdit

```html
<!DOCTYPE html>
<html>
<head>
    <title>{% block title %}Django Blog{% endblock %}</title>
</head>
```

86

```html
<body>
    <header>
        <h1>My Django Blog</h1>
    </header>
    <main>
        {% block content %}{% endblock %}
    </main>
    <footer>
        <p>Copyright © 2025</p>
    </footer>
</body>
</html>
```

b) Extending the Base Template (home.html)

html

CopyEdit

```html
{% extends "base.html" %}


{% block title %}Home Page{% endblock %}


{% block content %}
    <h2>Welcome to the Blog</h2>
```

```
    <p>This is the homepage.</p>
```

`{% endblock %}`

Now, home.html inherits the structure from base.html, ensuring consistency across pages.

5. Using Static Files (CSS, JavaScript, Images)

Django manages static files (CSS, JS, images) using the static template tag.

a) Configure Static Files in settings.py

python

CopyEdit

```
STATIC_URL = '/static/'

STATICFILES_DIRS = [BASE_DIR / "static"]
```

b) Load Static Files in a Template

html

CopyEdit

```
{% load static %}

<link rel="stylesheet" href="{% static 'css/style.css' %}">

<img src="{% static 'images/logo.png' %}" alt="Logo">
```

Static files are stored in:

sql

CopyEdit

```
static/
|-- css/
|   |-- style.css
|-- images/
|   |-- logo.png
```

Template Inheritance and Reusability

In a typical web application, multiple pages often share common elements like headers, footers, and navigation bars. Instead of duplicating these elements in every template, Django provides template inheritance, which allows a base template to be extended by other templates.

1. Creating a Base Template (base.html)

A base template defines the common structure of the application. This includes elements like the header, footer, and main content area, where child templates can insert their content.

Example: base.html

html

CopyEdit

```
<!DOCTYPE html>
<html>
<head>
```

```html
<title>{% block title %}Django Application{% endblock %}</title>
{% load static %}
<link rel="stylesheet" href="{% static 'css/style.css' %}">
</head>
<body>
  <header>
    <h1>My Django Website</h1>
    <nav>
      <ul>
        <li><a href="{% url 'home' %}">Home</a></li>
        <li><a href="{% url 'about' %}">About</a></li>
        <li><a href="{% url 'contact' %}">Contact</a></li>
      </ul>
    </nav>
  </header>

  <main>
    {% block content %}{% endblock %}
  </main>

  <footer>
    <p>© 2025 My Django Website</p>
```

        </tooter>

</body>

</html>

2. Extending the Base Template (home.html)

Child templates inherit from base.html using {% extends %} and define specific content inside {% block %} tags.

Example: home.html

html

CopyEdit

{% extends "base.html" %}

{% block title %}Home - Django App{% endblock %}

{% block content %}

   <h2>Welcome to My Django Website</h2>

   <p>This is the home page.</p>
{% endblock %}

3. Creating Another Template (about.html)

Other pages, like an "About" page, can extend base.html and provide custom content.

91

Example: about.html

html

CopyEdit

{% extends "base.html" %}

{% block title %}About Us{% endblock %}

{% block content %}
  <h2>About Our Website</h2>
  <p>This website is built using Django.</p>
{% endblock %}

Now, when you visit /home/ or /about/, Django will render the correct page while keeping the shared structure intact.

4. Nesting Blocks for Further Customization

You can define multiple block sections in the base template for better customization.

Example: Adding a Sidebar in base.html

html

CopyEdit

<aside>
  {% block sidebar %}
    <p>Default Sidebar Content</p>

92

```
{% endblock %}
```

```
</aside>
```

A child template can override this block:

html

CopyEdit

```
{% block sidebar %}

   <ul>

      <li>Latest Posts</li>

      <li>Categories</li>

   </ul>

{% endblock %}
```

5. Using Template Includes for Reusable Components

For repeating sections like navigation bars and footers, use {% include %} **instead of inheritance.**

Example: Creating a Reusable Navigation Bar (navbar.html)

html

CopyEdit

```
<nav>

   <ul>

      <li><a href="{% url 'home' %}">Home</a></li>

      <li><a href="{% url 'about' %}">About</a></li>
```

```
<li><a href="{% url 'contact' %}">Contact</a></li>

  </ul>

</nav>
```

Include it in base.html:

html

CopyEdit

```
{% include "navbar.html" %}
```

This method avoids duplicate code while keeping the structure modular.

Static and Media Files in Django

Django handles two types of non-database files:

- **Static Files (CSS, JavaScript, images) – Required for website styling and functionality.**
- **Media Files (User-uploaded files) – Uploaded images, PDFs, and other assets.**

1. Managing Static Files (CSS, JavaScript, Images)

a) Configuring Static Files in settings.py

python

CopyEdit

```
STATIC_URL = '/static/'
```

```
STATICFILES_DIRS = [BASE_DIR / "static"]
```

b) Creating a Static Directory Structure

lua

CopyEdit

```
myapp/
|-- static/
|   |-- css/
|   |   |-- style.css
|   |-- js/
|   |   |-- script.js
|   |-- images/
|       |-- logo.png
```

c) Loading Static Files in Templates

html

CopyEdit

```
{% load static %}
<link rel="stylesheet" href="{% static 'css/style.css' %}">
<script src="{% static 'js/script.js' %}"></script>
<img src="{% static 'images/logo.png' %}" alt="Logo">
```

95

Now, Django will serve these files whenever they are requested.

2. Using Static Files in Views

You can programmatically reference static files in views:

python

CopyEdit

```
from django.templatetags.static import static


logo_url = static('images/logo.png')
```

This generates /static/images/logo.png, **which can be used in JavaScript or APIs.**

3. Serving Media Files (User Uploads)

Media files are different from static files because they are uploaded by users.

a) Configure Media File Handling in settings.py

python

CopyEdit

```
MEDIA_URL = '/media/'

MEDIA_ROOT = BASE_DIR / "media"
```

b) Updating urls.py to Serve Media Files

python

CopyEdit

```python
from django.conf import settings
from django.conf.urls.static import static

urlpatterns = [
    # Other URL patterns
] + static(settings.MEDIA_URL, document_root=settings.MEDIA_ROOT)
```

c) Creating an Upload Model

For user-uploaded files like profile pictures:

python

CopyEdit

```python
from django.db import models

class UserProfile(models.Model):
    name = models.CharField(max_length=100)
    profile_picture = models.ImageField(upload_to='profile_pics/')

    def __str__(self):
        return self.name
```

97

d) Handling File Uploads in Forms

python

CopyEdit

```python
from django import forms
from .models import UserProfile


class ProfileForm(forms.ModelForm):
    class Meta:
        model = UserProfile
        fields = ['name', 'profile_picture']
```

e) Displaying Uploaded Images in Templates

html

CopyEdit

```html
<img src="{{ user.profile_picture.url }}" alt="Profile Picture">
```

4. Collecting Static Files for Production

In development, Django serves static files automatically, but in production, you must collect all static files into a single directory.

Run the following command:

sh

CopyEdit

```sh
python manage.py collectstatic
```

98

This gathers all static files into STATIC_ROOT, making them ready for deployment.

Chapter 5: Working with Forms in Django

Forms are an essential part of web applications, allowing users to input and submit data. Django provides a **powerful form-handling mechanism** that simplifies user input validation, data processing, and security. The Django Forms framework eliminates repetitive code and ensures safe handling of form data.

Introduction to Django Forms

Django Forms provide a **structured and secure way** to handle user input. They integrate with Django's **Model Forms (forms tied to database models)** and **Standard Forms (independent from models)**.

Why Use Django Forms?

- **Automatic Data Validation** – Ensures user input is correctly formatted.
- **Cross-Site Request Forgery (CSRF) Protection** – Prevents malicious form submissions.
- **Reusability** – Forms can be reused across different views.
- **Integration with Models** – Allows seamless interaction with the database.

2. Creating a Basic Django Form

Django provides a built-in forms module that allows creating forms easily.

Example: Creating a Contact Form

Create a forms.py file inside your Django app:

```python
CopyEdit
from django import forms

class ContactForm(forms.Form):
    name = forms.CharField(max_length=100)
    email = forms.EmailField()
    message = forms.CharField(widget=forms.Textarea)
```

- CharField – Handles short text input.
- EmailField – Validates email input.
- Textarea Widget – Displays a multi-line text box.

Rendering the Form in a View

Open views.py and add:

python
CopyEdit
```python
from django.shortcuts import render
from .forms import ContactForm

def contact_view(request):
    form = ContactForm()  # Create an empty form instance
    return render(request, 'contact.html', {'form': form})
```

Displaying the Form in a Template

Create contact.html:

html
CopyEdit
```html
<!DOCTYPE html>
<html>
<head>
    <title>Contact Us</title>
</head>
<body>
    <h2>Contact Us</h2>
    <form method="post">
        {% csrf_token %}
        {{ form.as_p }}
        <button type="submit">Submit</button>
    </form>
</body>
</html>
```

- {% csrf_token %} – Prevents **CSRF attacks** by securing form submissions.

101

- {{ form.as_p }} – Renders the form fields inside <p> tags.

Handling Form Submissions

When a user submits a form, Django **validates the input, processes the data, and returns a response**.

3.1 Handling POST Requests in Views

Modify contact_view to handle form submissions:

python
CopyEdit
```python
from django.http import HttpResponse
from django.shortcuts import render
from .forms import ContactForm

def contact_view(request):
    if request.method == "POST":
        form = ContactForm(request.POST)  # Bind submitted data to the form
        if form.is_valid():  # Validate input
            name = form.cleaned_data['name']
            email = form.cleaned_data['email']
            message = form.cleaned_data['message']
            return HttpResponse(f"Thank you, {name}! Your message has been received.")
    else:
        form = ContactForm()  # Display an empty form for GET requests

    return render(request, 'contact.html', {'form': form})
```

- request.POST – Contains **submitted form data.**
- form.is_valid() – Checks if **input meets validation rules**.
- cleaned_data – Stores **validated form data.**

3.2 Improving the Form Template

Modify contact.html to display error messages:

html
CopyEdit
```
<form method="post">
  {% csrf_token %}
  {{ form.as_p }}

  {% if form.errors %}
    <ul>
      {% for field, errors in form.errors.items %}
        {% for error in errors %}
          <li>{{ field|title }}: {{ error }}</li>
        {% endfor %}
      {% endfor %}
    </ul>
  {% endif %}

  <button type="submit">Submit</button>
</form>
```

Now, if a user **enters an invalid email or leaves fields blank**, Django will display error messages.

4. Pre-Populating Forms with Initial Data

You can **pre-fill** a form with default values.

Example: Preloading User Data

python
CopyEdit
```
def contact_view(request):
    form = ContactForm(initial={'name': 'John Doe', 'email': 'johndoe@example.com'})
    return render(request, 'contact.html', {'form': form})
```

103

Now, when the page loads, the form will have **"John Doe"** and **"johndoe@example.com"** pre-filled.

5. Custom Form Validation

Django allows adding **custom validation logic**.

5.1 Validating a Name Field

Modify forms.py:

```python
CopyEdit
class ContactForm(forms.Form):
    name = forms.CharField(max_length=100)
    email = forms.EmailField()
    message = forms.CharField(widget=forms.Textarea)

    def clean_name(self):
        name = self.cleaned_data.get("name")
        if "admin" in name.lower():
            raise forms.ValidationError("The word 'admin' is not allowed in the name.")
        return name
```

Now, if a user enters **"admin"** in the name field, Django will reject the form.

6. Redirecting After Form Submission

Instead of displaying a success message on the same page, **redirect users to another page** after submitting the form.

Modify contact_view:

```python
CopyEdit
from django.shortcuts import redirect

def contact_view(request):
```

104

```
if request.method == "POST":
    form = ContactForm(request.POST)
    if form.is_valid():
        return redirect('success_page')  # Redirect to success page

else:
    form = ContactForm()

return render(request, 'contact.html', {'form': form})
```

Add a new success view:

python
CopyEdit
```
def success_view(request):
    return HttpResponse("Your message has been sent successfully!")
```

Map it in urls.py:

python
CopyEdit
```
from django.urls import path
from .views import contact_view, success_view

urlpatterns = [
    path('contact/', contact_view, name='contact'),
    path('success/', success_view, name='success_page'),
]
```

Now, after submitting the form, users are redirected to /success/.

Validating User Input and Handling Errors

Django's form validation system is designed to **automatically handle incorrect input** and provide feedback to users.

1.1 Built-in Field Validations

Django provides automatic validation for fields like:

- **Required fields** – Empty input is rejected.
- **Max and min length** – Restricts input length.
- **Email validation** – Ensures correct format.
- **Numeric fields** – Only accept numbers.

Example: **Form with Built-in Validation**

python

CopyEdit

```python
from django import forms


class RegistrationForm(forms.Form):
    username = forms.CharField(max_length=30, required=True)
    email = forms.EmailField(required=True)
    age = forms.IntegerField(min_value=18, required=True)
```

Django automatically enforces:

- username must not exceed **30 characters**.
- email must be in **valid format**.
- age must be at least **18**.

If a user submits invalid data, Django generates **error messages**.

1.2 Displaying Validation Errors in Templates

Modify views.py to handle form errors:

python

CopyEdit

```python
from django.shortcuts import render
from .forms import RegistrationForm

def register_view(request):
    if request.method == "POST":
        form = RegistrationForm(request.POST)
        if form.is_valid():
            return render(request, 'success.html')  # Redirect on success
    else:
        form = RegistrationForm()

    return render(request, 'register.html', {'form': form})
```

In register.html, display error messages:

html

CopyEdit

```html
<form method="post">
    {% csrf_token %}
```

107

```
{{ form.as_p }}

{% if form.errors %}
    <ul>
        {% for field, errors in form.errors.items %}
            {% for error in errors %}
                <li>{{ field|title }}: {{ error }}</li>
            {% endfor %}
        {% endfor %}
    </ul>
{% endif %}


    <button type="submit">Register</button>
</form>
```

Now, if a user **misses a required field or enters invalid data**, Django will display error messages.

1.3 Custom Validation with clean_<field> Method

Sometimes, built-in validation is not enough. You can add **custom validation** using clean_<field>().

Example: Restricting Username Format

python

CopyEdit

```python
class RegistrationForm(forms.Form):
    username = forms.CharField(max_length=30)
    email = forms.EmailField()

    def clean_username(self):
        username = self.cleaned_data['username']
        if "admin" in username.lower():
            raise forms.ValidationError("Username cannot contain 'admin'.")
        return username
```

If a user enters **"admin123"**, Django will **reject the input**.

1.4 Validating Multiple Fields (clean())

If validation depends on **multiple fields**, override clean().

Example: Password Confirmation

python

CopyEdit

```python
class RegistrationForm(forms.Form):
    password = forms.CharField(widget=forms.PasswordInput)
```

109

```python
confirm_password = forms.CharField(widget=forms.PasswordInput)

def clean(self):
    cleaned_data = super().clean()
    password = cleaned_data.get("password")
    confirm_password = cleaned_data.get("confirm_password")

    if password and confirm_password and password != confirm_password:
        raise forms.ValidationError("Passwords do not match.")
```

If passwords **don't match**, Django will display an **error message**.

Creating Custom Form Fields and Widgets

Django allows **customizing form fields and widgets** to improve **validation and user experience**.

2.1 Custom Form Fields

Django's forms.Field class can be extended to create **custom fields**.

Example: Creating a Phone Number Field

python

CopyEdit

```python
import re
from django import forms
```

```python
class PhoneNumberField(forms.CharField):
    def validate(self, value):
        super().validate(value)  # Default validation
        if not re.match(r'^\+?\d{10,15}$', value):
            raise forms.ValidationError("Enter a valid phone number.")
```

Now, use this field in a form:

python

CopyEdit

```python
class ContactForm(forms.Form):
    name = forms.CharField(max_length=100)
    phone = PhoneNumberField()
```

If the phone number **doesn't match the pattern**, Django will reject it.

2.2 Customizing Form Widgets

Widgets **control the appearance of form fields** in templates. Django provides widgets like:

- TextInput – Standard input field.
- Textarea – Multi-line input field.
- Select – Dropdown list.
- RadioSelect – Radio buttons.

Example: Customizing Widgets in a Form

python

CopyEdit

```python
class ContactForm(forms.Form):
    name = forms.CharField(widget=forms.TextInput(attrs={'class': 'form-control'}))
    message = forms.CharField(widget=forms.Textarea(attrs={'rows': 4, 'cols': 40}))
    contact_method = forms.ChoiceField(
        choices=[('email', 'Email'), ('phone', 'Phone')],
        widget=forms.RadioSelect
    )
```

2.3 Rendering Custom Widgets in Templates

In contact.html:

html

CopyEdit

```html
<form method="post">
    {% csrf_token %}

    <label for="id_name">Name:</label>
    {{ form.name }}

    <label for="id_message">Message:</label>
```

112

```
{{ form.message }}

<label>Contact Method:</label>

{{ form.contact_method }}


  <button type="submit">Submit</button>
</form>
```

Now, the form will have:

- A **styled text input** for name.
- A **textarea** for messages.
- **Radio buttons** for selecting contact method.

2.4 Using Custom Widgets for Date Input

Django's default date input field is **not user-friendly**. Use DateInput with a date picker.

Modify forms.py:

python

CopyEdit

```python
class EventForm(forms.Form):

    event_name = forms.CharField()

    event_date = forms.DateField(widget=forms.DateInput(attrs={'type': 'date'}))
```

Now, the browser will show a **calendar pop-up** for selecting dates.

113

3. Using Django's widgets.py for Reusable Custom Widgets

Instead of defining widgets in a form, you can **create a separate** widgets.py **file** for reuse.

Create widgets.py:

python

CopyEdit

```python
from django.forms import TextInput


class CustomTextInput(TextInput):
    def __init__(self, *args, **kwargs):
        kwargs.setdefault('attrs', {}).update({'class': 'custom-input'})
        super().__init__(*args, **kwargs)
```

Use it in a form:

python

CopyEdit

```python
from .widgets import CustomTextInput


class CustomForm(forms.Form):
    name = forms.CharField(widget=CustomTextInput())
```

Now, all text fields **use the same custom styling**.

ModelForms: Automatically Generating Forms from Models

Django **ModelForms** bridge the gap between **models** and **forms**, ensuring that data validation, structure, and constraints remain **consistent** across the application.

1.1 Why Use ModelForms?

■ **Less Code** – Automatically creates form fields from models.
■ **Data Consistency** – Avoids mismatched form fields and database models.
■ **Built-in Validation** – Uses model constraints (e.g., max_length, unique).
■ **Direct Saving to Database** – Forms can be saved using .save().

1.2 Creating a ModelForm

Step 1: Define a Django Model

Open models.py and define a BlogPost model:

```python
CopyEdit
from django.db import models

class BlogPost(models.Model):
    title = models.CharField(max_length=255)
    content = models.TextField()
    author = models.CharField(max_length=100)
    created_at = models.DateTimeField(auto_now_add=True)

    def __str__(self):
        return self.title
```

Step 2: Create a ModelForm

Inside forms.py, define a ModelForm:

```python
CopyEdit
from django import forms
```

115

```
from .models import BlogPost

class BlogPostForm(forms.ModelForm):
    class Meta:
        model = BlogPost  # Link to BlogPost model
        fields = ['title', 'content', 'author']  # Fields to include in the form
```

- model = BlogPost – Tells Django **which model** the form is based on.
- fields = ['title', 'content', 'author'] – Specifies **which fields** to include.

You can also exclude fields using exclude:

python
CopyEdit
```
class BlogPostForm(forms.ModelForm):
    class Meta:
        model = BlogPost
        exclude = ['created_at']  # Excludes this field from the form
```

Step 3: Creating a View for Handling the Form

Modify views.py to **display and process the form**:

python
CopyEdit
```
from django.shortcuts import render, redirect
from .forms import BlogPostForm

def create_blog_post(request):
    if request.method == "POST":
        form = BlogPostForm(request.POST)  # Bind submitted data
        if form.is_valid():
            form.save()  # Save form data to database
            return redirect('success_page')  # Redirect on success
    else:
        form = BlogPostForm()
```

116

```
return render(request, 'blog_form.html', {'form': form})
```

Step 4: Creating the Template (blog_form.html)

html
CopyEdit

```
<form method="post">
    {% csrf_token %}
    {{ form.as_p }}  <!-- Renders form fields -->
    <button type="submit">Submit</button>
</form>
```

Now, when users **submit the form**, the blog post is saved **directly into the database**.

1.3 Customizing ModelForm Fields

By default, Django uses **standard form fields** based on the model. However, you can **override fields** to change their attributes.

Example: Customizing the content field

python
CopyEdit

```
class BlogPostForm(forms.ModelForm):
    content = forms.CharField(widget=forms.Textarea(attrs={'rows': 5}))

    class Meta:
        model = BlogPost
        fields = ['title', 'content', 'author']
```

Now, the **content field** will use a **larger text area**.

1.4 Adding Custom Validation in ModelForms

Django allows adding **validation logic** inside a ModelForm.

Example: Restricting Title Length

python
CopyEdit

```
class BlogPostForm(forms.ModelForm):
    class Meta:
        model = BlogPost
        fields = ['title', 'content', 'author']

    def clean_title(self):
        title = self.cleaned_data.get("title")
        if len(title) < 10:
            raise forms.ValidationError("Title must be at least 10 characters long.")
        return title
```

If a user enters a **short title**, Django **rejects the submission**.

File Uploads in Django

Django provides **built-in support for handling file uploads,** making it easy to store and manage **images, documents, and other file types**.

2.1 Configuring Django for File Uploads

Step 1: Update settings.py

Add MEDIA_URL and MEDIA_ROOT:

python
CopyEdit

```
MEDIA_URL = '/media/'
MEDIA_ROOT = BASE_DIR / "media"
```

These settings define where **uploaded files** will be stored.

Step 2: Update urls.py to Serve Media Files

Modify urls.py to **serve media files during development**:

python
CopyEdit
```
from django.conf import settings
from django.conf.urls.static import static

urlpatterns = [
    # Other URL patterns
] + static(settings.MEDIA_URL, document_root=settings.MEDIA_ROOT)
```

2.2 Creating a Model for File Uploads

Modify models.py to include an **image field**:

python
CopyEdit
```
class UserProfile(models.Model):
    name = models.CharField(max_length=100)
    profile_picture = models.ImageField(upload_to='profile_pics/')

    def __str__(self):
        return self.name
```

- upload_to='profile_pics/' – **Stores images in the** media/profile_pics/ directory.

2.3 Creating a ModelForm for File Uploads

In forms.py:

python
CopyEdit
```
class UserProfileForm(forms.ModelForm):
    class Meta:
```

119

```
model = UserProfile
fields = ['name', 'profile_picture']
```

2.4 Creating a View for Handling File Uploads

Modify views.py:

python
CopyEdit
```
def upload_profile_picture(request):
    if request.method == "POST":
        form = UserProfileForm(request.POST, request.FILES)  # Handle file uploads
        if form.is_valid():
            form.save()
            return redirect('success_page')
    else:
        form = UserProfileForm()

    return render(request, 'upload.html', {'form': form})
```

- request.FILES – Contains uploaded **file data**.

2.5 Creating the Upload Form Template (upload.html)

html
CopyEdit
```
<form method="post" enctype="multipart/form-data">
    {% csrf_token %}
    {{ form.as_p }}
    <button type="submit">Upload</button>
</form>
```

- **enctype="multipart/form-data"** is required for **file uploads**.

120

Now, users can **upload profile pictures**, and Django will store them in the /media/profile_pics/ directory.

2.6 Displaying Uploaded Files in Templates

Modify profile.html:

html
CopyEdit

```
<img src="{{ user.profile_picture.url }}" alt="Profile Picture">
```

Now, Django dynamically displays **uploaded profile pictures**.

2.7 Restricting File Types and Sizes

You can enforce **file type and size restrictions** using clean_<field>().

Modify UserProfileForm:

python
CopyEdit

```
from django.core.exceptions import ValidationError

def validate_file_size(value):
    limit = 5 * 1024 * 1024  # 5MB limit
    if value.size > limit:
        raise ValidationError("File size must be under 5MB.")

class UserProfileForm(forms.ModelForm):
    profile_picture = forms.ImageField(validators=[validate_file_size])

    class Meta:
        model = UserProfile
        fields = ['name', 'profile_picture']
```

121

Now, if users upload files **larger than 5MB**, Django will reject them.

Key Takeaways

■ **ModelForms Automatically Generate Forms from Models** – Reduces redundancy and maintains consistency.

■ **Form Data Can Be Directly Saved to the Database** – Using .save() ensures seamless model integration.

■ **File Uploads Are Handled with** request.FILES – Required for handling images, PDFs, and documents.

■ **Media Files Must Be Configured in** settings.py **and** urls.py – Ensures proper storage and retrieval.

■ **Custom Validation Can Restrict File Size and Type** – Prevents users from uploading invalid files.

Django's **ModelForms and file handling** streamline **data input, validation, and storage**, making it easy to build feature-rich web applications.

Chapter 6: User Authentication and Authorization

Authentication and authorization are fundamental parts of any web application that requires user management. Django provides a **built-in authentication system** that handles **user login, registration, password management, and permissions** efficiently.

Django's Built-in Authentication System

Django's authentication system is a **fully-featured user management framework** that provides:

- **User authentication (login/logout)**
- **User registration and password hashing**
- **User groups and permissions**
- **Session management**

1.1 Enabling Django's Authentication System

Django's authentication system is included by default in INSTALLED_APPS:

```python
CopyEdit
INSTALLED_APPS = [
    'django.contrib.auth',  # Enables authentication system
    'django.contrib.contenttypes',
    'django.contrib.sessions',
]
```

Ensure that AUTHENTICATION_BACKENDS is set to use Django's authentication system:

```python
CopyEdit
AUTHENTICATION_BACKENDS = [
    'django.contrib.auth.backends.ModelBackend',
]
```

1.2 User Model Overview

Django provides a default User model that includes:

- **Username and email fields**
- **Password hashing and authentication**
- **Permissions and groups**

You can access the built-in User model as follows:

python
CopyEdit
```python
from django.contrib.auth.models import User
```

To create a user manually:

python
CopyEdit
```python
user = User.objects.create_user(username='john_doe', email='john@example.com', password='securepassword')
```

Django automatically **hashes passwords**, ensuring security.

1.3 User Registration with Django's Authentication System

Step 1: Create a User Registration Form

In forms.py:

python
CopyEdit
```python
from django import forms
from django.contrib.auth.models import User

class UserRegistrationForm(forms.ModelForm):
    password = forms.CharField(widget=forms.PasswordInput)
    confirm_password = forms.CharField(widget=forms.PasswordInput)
```

```python
class Meta:
    model = User
    fields = ['username', 'email', 'password']

def clean(self):
    cleaned_data = super().clean()
    password = cleaned_data.get("password")
    confirm_password = cleaned_data.get("confirm_password")

    if password != confirm_password:
        raise forms.ValidationError("Passwords do not match.")
```

Step 2: Create a Registration View

In views.py:

python
CopyEdit
```python
from django.shortcuts import render, redirect
from django.contrib.auth import login
from .forms import UserRegistrationForm

def register_view(request):
    if request.method == "POST":
        form = UserRegistrationForm(request.POST)
        if form.is_valid():
            user = form.save(commit=False)
            user.set_password(form.cleaned_data['password'])  # Hash password
            user.save()
            login(request, user)  # Auto-login user
            return redirect('home')
    else:
        form = UserRegistrationForm()

    return render(request, 'register.html', {'form': form})
```

Step 3: Create the Registration Template (register.html)

html
CopyEdit

```
<form method="post">
    {% csrf_token %}
    {{ form.as_p }}
    <button type="submit">Register</button>
</form>
```

Now, users can register, and their credentials will be **securely stored** in the database.

1.4 User Login and Logout

Django provides **built-in views** for login/logout.

Step 1: Configure Authentication URLs in urls.py

python
CopyEdit

```
from django.urls import path
from django.contrib.auth import views as auth_views

urlpatterns = [
    path('login/', auth_views.LoginView.as_view(template_name='login.html'),
name='login'),
    path('logout/', auth_views.LogoutView.as_view(), name='logout'),
]
```

Step 2: Create a Login Template (login.html)

html
CopyEdit

```
<form method="post">
    {% csrf_token %}
    <input type="text" name="username" placeholder="Username">
    <input type="password" name="password" placeholder="Password">
    <button type="submit">Login</button>
</form>
```

126

Now, visiting /login/ allows users to log in.

1.5 Restricting Access to Authenticated Users

Use @login_required to restrict views to **logged-in users only**.

python
CopyEdit
```python
from django.contrib.auth.decorators import login_required

@login_required
def dashboard(request):
    return render(request, 'dashboard.html')
```

For class-based views:

python
CopyEdit
```python
from django.contrib.auth.mixins import LoginRequiredMixin
from django.views.generic import TemplateView

class DashboardView(LoginRequiredMixin, TemplateView):
    template_name = "dashboard.html"
```

Django will **redirect unauthenticated users** to the login page.

Customizing the User Model

Django's default User model works well for most cases, but sometimes you need **additional fields** (e.g., profile picture, phone number).

Django provides two approaches for customizing the user model:

- AbstractUser – Extends Django's built-in User model while retaining its fields.

127

- **AbstractBaseUser** – Allows full customization of the user model.

2.1 Extending the Default User Model with AbstractUser

Use AbstractUser when you **want to add extra fields** without modifying core authentication functionality.

Step 1: Create a Custom User Model

In models.py:

python
CopyEdit
```python
from django.contrib.auth.models import AbstractUser
from django.db import models

class CustomUser(AbstractUser):
    phone_number = models.CharField(max_length=15, blank=True, null=True)
    profile_picture = models.ImageField(upload_to='profiles/', blank=True, null=True)
```

Step 2: Update settings.py to Use the Custom Model
python
CopyEdit
```python
AUTH_USER_MODEL = 'myapp.CustomUser'
```

Now, this model will **replace Django's default User model**.

2.2 Fully Customizing the User Model with AbstractBaseUser

Use AbstractBaseUser when **you want full control** over authentication fields (e.g., removing usernames in favor of email-based login).

Step 1. Define a Custom User Model

python
CopyEdit

```python
from django.contrib.auth.models import AbstractBaseUser, BaseUserManager
from django.db import models

class CustomUserManager(BaseUserManager):
    def create_user(self, email, password=None):
        if not email:
            raise ValueError("Users must have an email address")
        user = self.model(email=self.normalize_email(email))
        user.set_password(password)
        user.save(using=self._db)
        return user

    def create_superuser(self, email, password):
        user = self.create_user(email, password)
        user.is_admin = True
        user.save(using=self._db)
        return user

class CustomUser(AbstractBaseUser):
    email = models.EmailField(unique=True)
    full_name = models.CharField(max_length=150)
    is_active = models.BooleanField(default=True)
    is_admin = models.BooleanField(default=False)

    objects = CustomUserManager()

    USERNAME_FIELD = 'email'  # Use email instead of username
    REQUIRED_FIELDS = ['full_name']
```

Step 2: Update settings.py

python
CopyEdit

```python
AUTH_USER_MODEL = 'myapp.CustomUser'
```

129

Now, users **log in with their email instead of username**.

Implementing User Registration and Login Functionality

Django provides a built-in user authentication system, making it **easy to manage user accounts**.

1.1 User Registration (Sign-Up)

Step 1: Create a User Registration Form

Modify forms.py to define a **user registration form**:

python

CopyEdit

```python
from django import forms
from django.contrib.auth.models import User


class UserRegistrationForm(forms.ModelForm):
    password = forms.CharField(widget=forms.PasswordInput)
    confirm_password = forms.CharField(widget=forms.PasswordInput)


    class Meta:
        model = User
        fields = ['username', 'email', 'password']
```

```python
def clean(self):
    cleaned_data = super().clean()
    password = cleaned_data.get("password")
    confirm_password = cleaned_data.get("confirm_password")

    if password and confirm_password and password != confirm_password:
        raise forms.ValidationError("Passwords do not match.")
```

- password = forms.CharField(widget=forms.PasswordInput) ensures passwords are **masked**.
- clean() method validates that **passwords match**.

Step 2: Create a Registration View

Modify views.py:

python

CopyEdit

```python
from django.shortcuts import render, redirect
from django.contrib.auth import login
from .forms import UserRegistrationForm

def register_view(request):
    if request.method == "POST":
        form = UserRegistrationForm(request.POST)
```

```python
if form.is_valid():

    user = form.save(commit=False)

    user.set_password(form.cleaned_data['password'])  # Hash password

    user.save()

    login(request, user)  # Automatically log in the user

    return redirect('home')

else:

    form = UserRegistrationForm()


return render(request, 'register.html', {'form': form})
```

- user.set_password() ensures **secure password storage**.
- login(request, user) automatically **logs in** the user after registration.

Step 3: Create the Registration Template (register.html)

html

CopyEdit

```html
<form method="post">

    {% csrf_token %}

    {{ form.as_p }}

    <button type="submit">Register</button>

</form>
```

132

Now, users can **register** and their credentials will be **securely stored**.

1.2 User Login and Logout

Django provides built-in **views for authentication,** making login and logout **simple to implement**.

Step 1: Add Login and Logout URLs in urls.py

python

CopyEdit

```python
from django.urls import path

from django.contrib.auth import views as auth_views


urlpatterns = [

    path('login/', auth_views.LoginView.as_view(template_name='login.html'),
name='login'),

    path('logout/', auth_views.LogoutView.as_view(), name='logout'),

]
```

Step 2: Create the Login Template (login.html)

html

CopyEdit

```html
<form method="post">

    {% csrf_token %}

    <input type="text" name="username" placeholder="Username">
```

133

```html
<input type="password" name="password" placeholder="Password">
<button type="submit">Login</button>
</form>
```

Step 3: Restrict Views to Authenticated Users

Use @login_required to **protect views from unauthorized access**:

python

CopyEdit

```python
from django.contrib.auth.decorators import login_required


@login_required
def dashboard(request):
    return render(request, 'dashboard.html')
```

For **class-based views,** use LoginRequiredMixin:

python

CopyEdit

```python
from django.contrib.auth.mixins import LoginRequiredMixin
from django.views.generic import TemplateView


class DashboardView(LoginRequiredMixin, TemplateView):
    template_name = "dashboard.html"
```

134

- Unauthenticated users are **redirected to the login page**.

Password Hashing and Resetting Mechanism

Django uses **secure password hashing** to store user passwords, preventing them from being stored in plaintext.

2.1 How Django Hashes Passwords

Django automatically hashes passwords using the **PBKDF2 algorithm** by default. Other supported algorithms include **Argon2, bcrypt, and SHA-1**.

To check which algorithm is used:

python

CopyEdit

```
from django.contrib.auth.hashers import get_hasher

print(get_hasher().algorithm)  # Output: pbkdf2_sha256
```

2.2 Changing the Default Password Hasher

Modify settings.py:

python

CopyEdit

```
PASSWORD_HASHERS = [

    'django.contrib.auth.hashers.Argon2PasswordHasher',

    'django.contrib.auth.hashers.PBKDF2PasswordHasher',

]
```

135

Argon2 is recommended for **stronger security**.

2.3 Implementing Password Reset Mechanism

Django provides **built-in views** for password resets.

Step 1: Configure Email Settings in settings.py

Django sends password reset links via email:

python

CopyEdit

```
EMAIL_BACKEND = 'django.core.mail.backends.smtp.EmailBackend'

EMAIL_HOST = 'smtp.gmail.com'

EMAIL_PORT = 587

EMAIL_USE_TLS = True

EMAIL_HOST_USER = 'your-email@gmail.com'

EMAIL_HOST_PASSWORD = 'your-email-password'
```


For testing, use Django's **console backend**:

python

CopyEdit

```
EMAIL_BACKEND = 'django.core.mail.backends.console.EmailBackend'
```

Step 2: Add Password Reset URLs

Modify urls.py:

python

CopyEdit

```python
urlpatterns += [

    path('password_reset/', auth_views.PasswordResetView.as_view(),
name='password_reset'),

    path('password_reset/done/', auth_views.PasswordResetDoneView.as_view(),
name='password_reset_done'),

    path('reset/<uidb64>/<token>/', auth_views.PasswordResetConfirmView.as_view(),
name='password_reset_confirm'),

    path('reset/done/', auth_views.PasswordResetCompleteView.as_view(),
name='password_reset_complete'),

]
```

Django now **handles password reset flow automatically**.

Step 3: Create Password Reset Template (password_reset_form.html)

html

CopyEdit

```html
<form method="post">

    {% csrf_token %}

    <input type="email" name="email" placeholder="Enter your email">

    <button type="submit">Reset Password</button>
```

```
</form>
```

Once the email is submitted, Django sends a **password reset link**.

Step 4: Reset Password Confirmation Template (password_reset_confirm.html)

html

CopyEdit

```
<form method="post">
    {% csrf_token %}
    <input type="password" name="new_password1" placeholder="New Password">
    <input type="password" name="new_password2" placeholder="Confirm Password">
    <button type="submit">Change Password</button>
</form>
```

Once confirmed, the user's password is **securely updated**.

2.4 Changing Password from Profile (Without Reset Link)

If a logged-in user wants to **change their password**, Django provides:

Step 1: Add URL for Changing Password

python

CopyEdit

```
urlpatterns += [
```

138

```
    path('password_change/', auth_views.PasswordChangeView.as_view(),
name='password_change'),

    path('password_change/done/', auth_views.PasswordChangeDoneView.as_view(),
name='password_change_done'),

]
```

Step 2: Create a Password Change Template (password_change_form.html)

html

CopyEdit

```
<form method="post">

    {% csrf_token %}

    <input type="password" name="old_password" placeholder="Current Password">

    <input type="password" name="new_password1" placeholder="New Password">

    <input type="password" name="new_password2" placeholder="Confirm New
Password">

    <button type="submit">Change Password</button>

</form>
```

Django will **update the password securely**.

Social Authentication with OAuth (Google, Facebook, GitHub)

Django does not provide social authentication out of the box, but the **django-allauth**
package simplifies OAuth-based authentication for multiple providers.

1.1 Installing django-allauth

Run the following command:

sh

CopyEdit

```
pip install django-allauth
```

1.2 Configuring django-allauth in Django

Step 1: Add allauth to INSTALLED_APPS

Modify settings.py:

python

CopyEdit

```
INSTALLED_APPS = [

    'django.contrib.sites',  # Required for allauth

    'allauth',

    'allauth.account',

    'allauth.socialaccount',

    'allauth.socialaccount.providers.google',  # Enable Google authentication

    'allauth.socialaccount.providers.github',  # Enable GitHub authentication

    'allauth.socialaccount.providers.facebook',  # Enable Facebook authentication

]
```

Set Django's site ID.

python

CopyEdit

```
SITE_ID = 1
```

Enable authentication backends:

python

CopyEdit

```
AUTHENTICATION_BACKENDS = [

    'django.contrib.auth.backends.ModelBackend',

    'allauth.account.auth_backends.AuthenticationBackend',

]
```

Enable account settings:

python

CopyEdit

```
ACCOUNT_AUTHENTICATION_METHOD = "username_email"

ACCOUNT_EMAIL_REQUIRED = True

ACCOUNT_USERNAME_REQUIRED = True

ACCOUNT_EMAIL_VERIFICATION = "optional"
```

141

1.3 Setting Up OAuth for Google, Facebook, and GitHub

Each provider (Google, Facebook, GitHub) requires **OAuth credentials**.

Google OAuth Setup

1. Go to the Google Cloud Console.
2. Create a new project.
3. Enable **OAuth consent screen**.
4. Generate **OAuth client ID** and **secret**.
5. Add http://localhost:8000/accounts/google/login/callback/ as an **Authorized Redirect URI**.
6. Copy **Client ID and Secret**.

Facebook OAuth Setup

1. Go to Facebook Developers Console.
2. Create an **App ID**.
3. Enable **OAuth login**.
4. Add http://localhost:8000/accounts/facebook/login/callback/ as a **redirect URI**.
5. Copy **App ID and App Secret**.

GitHub OAuth Setup

1. Go to GitHub Developer Settings.
2. Register a new **OAuth application**.
3. Set http://localhost:8000/accounts/github/login/callback/ as the **callback URL**.
4. Copy **Client ID and Secret**.

1.4 Configuring OAuth Providers in Django

Add credentials to settings.py:

python

CopyEdit

```
SOCIALACCOUNT_PROVIDERS = {

  'google': {
```

```
    'APP': {

      'client_id': "GOOGLE_CLIENT_ID",

      'secret': "GOOGLE_SECRET",

      'key': "",

    }

  },

  'github': {

    'APP': {

      'client_id': "GITHUB_CLIENT_ID",

      'secret': "GITHUB_SECRET",

      'key': "",

    }

  },

  'facebook': {

    'APP': {

      'client_id': "FACEBOOK_APP_ID",

      'secret': "FACEBOOK_APP_SECRET",

      'key': "",

    }

  }

}
```

1.5 Adding Social Login URLs

Modify urls.py:

python

CopyEdit

```
from django.urls import path, include


urlpatterns = [
    path('accounts/', include('allauth.urls')),  # Allauth routes
]
```

Now, Django automatically generates **login URLs**:

- **Google Login:** /accounts/google/login/
- **Facebook Login:** /accounts/facebook/login/
- **GitHub Login:** /accounts/github/login/

1.6 Adding Social Login Buttons to Template

Modify login.html:

html

CopyEdit

```
<a href="{% provider_login_url 'google' %}">Login with Google</a>

<a href="{% provider_login_url 'github' %}">Login with GitHub</a>

<a href="{% provider_login_url 'facebook' %}">Login with Facebook</a>
```

Now, users can **log in using social accounts**.

Role-Based Access Control (RBAC) and Permissions

Role-Based Access Control (RBAC) is a **security model** that assigns permissions to users based on roles.

Django has **built-in user permissions and groups** that help implement RBAC.

2.1 Understanding Django's Permissions System

Django automatically creates **default permissions** for models:

- add_<modelname>
- change_<modelname>
- delete_<modelname>
- view_<modelname>

Example:
For a BlogPost model, Django generates:

- add_blogpost
- change_blogpost
- delete_blogpost
- view_blogpost

To check a user's permissions:

python

CopyEdit

```
if request.user.has_perm('app_name.add_blogpost'):

    print("User has permission to add blog posts")
```

2.2 Managing Permissions in Django Admin

1. Go to /admin/ and open **Users**.
2. Select a user and **assign permissions**.
3. Users can now access **specific admin sections** based on permissions.

2.3 Creating User Groups (Admin, Editor, Viewer)

Django **Groups** allow assigning multiple permissions to users.

Step 1: Create User Groups in Django Admin

1. Go to **Admin Panel → Groups**.
2. Create groups:
   - **Admin** (Full permissions)
   - **Editor** (Can edit, cannot delete)
   - **Viewer** (Read-only access)
3. Assign **permissions** to each group.

Step 2: Assign Users to Groups

python

CopyEdit

```python
from django.contrib.auth.models import Group, User


editor_group = Group.objects.get(name='Editor')

user = User.objects.get(username='john_doe')

user.groups.add(editor_group)
```

Now, john_doe is part of the **Editor group**.

146

2.4 Restricting Access Based on Roles

Using @permission_required Decorator

python

CopyEdit

```python
from django.contrib.auth.decorators import permission_required


@permission_required('app_name.change_blogpost')
def edit_blog_post(request):
    return HttpResponse("You have permission to edit blog posts.")
```

Using Django's user_passes_test Decorator

Restrict access to admins only:

python

CopyEdit

```python
from django.contrib.auth.decorators import user_passes_test


def is_admin(user):
    return user.is_superuser


@user_passes_test(is_admin)
def admin_dashboard(request):
    return HttpResponse("Admin Dashboard")
```

147

Restricting Access in Templates

html

CopyEdit

```
{% if perms.app_name.change_blogpost %}
    <a href="{% url 'edit_post' %}">Edit Post</a>
{% endif %}
```

2.5 Implementing Role-Based Dashboard

Views (views.py)

python

CopyEdit

```python
from django.contrib.auth.decorators import login_required

@login_required
def dashboard(request):
    if request.user.groups.filter(name="Admin").exists():
        return render(request, 'admin_dashboard.html')
    elif request.user.groups.filter(name="Editor").exists():
        return render(request, 'editor_dashboard.html')
    else:
        return render(request, 'viewer_dashboard.html')
```

148

URLs (urls.py)

python

CopyEdit

```python
urlpatterns += [
    path('dashboard/', dashboard, name='dashboard'),
]
```

Key Takeaways

■ **Django Supports OAuth via django-allauth** – Easily integrates **Google, Facebook, GitHub login**.

■ **RBAC Manages User Permissions** – Assign roles like **Admin, Editor, Viewer**.

■ **Django Provides Built-in Permissions** – Check permissions with has_perm().

■ **Groups Simplify Role Assignments** – Users inherit permissions from groups.

■ **Restrict Views and Templates Based on Roles** – Control access using decorators.

Chapter 7: Django REST Framework (DRF) – Building APIs

Django REST Framework (DRF) is a **powerful toolkit** for building **RESTful APIs** using Django. It provides flexible features for **authentication, serialization, and API views**, making it the preferred choice for developing APIs in Django applications.

Introduction to RESTful APIs and Django REST Framework

1.1 What is a RESTful API?

A **RESTful API (Representational State Transfer API)** follows a set of design principles to enable communication between clients and servers over HTTP. It provides **data exchange in JSON or XML format** using standard HTTP methods:

HTTP Method	CRUD Operation	Example API Endpoint
GET	Read	/api/posts/ (Fetch all posts)
POST	Create	/api/posts/ (Create a new post)
PUT/PATCH	Update	/api/posts/1/ (Update post with ID 1)
DELETE	Delete	/api/posts/1/ (Delete post with ID 1)

REST APIs allow **stateless communication**, meaning each request **contains all necessary information** without relying on previous requests.

1.2 Why Use Django REST Framework (DRF)?

Django REST Framework extends Django to simplify API development with features like:

■ **Serialization** – Converts Python objects (querysets, models) into JSON.
■ **Authentication & Permissions** – Supports token-based authentication and access control.
■ **Browsable API Interface** – Provides a web UI for API testing.
■ **Pagination & Filtering** – Handles large datasets efficiently.
■ **Throttling & Rate Limiting** – Prevents excessive API requests.

1.3 Installing Django REST Framework

Install DRF using pip:

sh
CopyEdit
```
pip install djangorestframework
```

Add rest_framework to INSTALLED_APPS in settings.py:

python
CopyEdit
```
INSTALLED_APPS = [
  'rest_framework',
]
```

Configure **default settings** for DRF:

python
CopyEdit
```
REST_FRAMEWORK = {
  'DEFAULT_AUTHENTICATION_CLASSES': [
    'rest_framework.authentication.SessionAuthentication',
    'rest_framework.authentication.TokenAuthentication',
  ],
  'DEFAULT_PERMISSION_CLASSES': [
    'rest_framework.permissions.AllowAny',  # Change to IsAuthenticated for restricted access
  ]
}
```

Now, DRF is set up and ready for building APIs.

Creating API Views: Function-Based vs. Class-Based API Views

Django REST Framework allows API views to be created using **Function-Based Views (FBVs)** and **Class-Based Views (CBVs)**.

2.1 Function-Based API Views (FBVs)

FBVs use Django's traditional **view functions** with DRF's @api_view decorator.

Example: Simple API View (FBV)

Create a basic API endpoint in views.py:

python
CopyEdit
```python
from rest_framework.decorators import api_view
from rest_framework.response import Response

@api_view(['GET'])
def api_home(request):
    return Response({"message": "Welcome to Django REST API!"})
```

- @api_view(['GET']) – Defines which HTTP methods the API supports.
- Response({...}) – Returns **JSON data**.

Mapping the View in urls.py
python
CopyEdit
```python
from django.urls import path
from .views import api_home

urlpatterns = [
    path('api/home/', api_home, name='api_home'),
]
```

Now, visiting /api/home/ will return:

json
CopyEdit

```
{
  "message": "Welcome to Django REST API!"
}
```

2.2 Handling CRUD Operations with Function-Based API Views

Let's create an API to manage **BlogPost** objects.

Step 1: Define a Django Model (models.py)
python
CopyEdit

```
from django.db import models

class BlogPost(models.Model):
    title = models.CharField(max_length=255)
    content = models.TextField()
    author = models.CharField(max_length=100)
    created_at = models.DateTimeField(auto_now_add=True)

    def __str__(self):
        return self.title
```

Step 2: Create a Serializer (serializers.py)

Serializers **convert model instances into JSON data**.

python
CopyEdit

```
from rest_framework import serializers
from .models import BlogPost

class BlogPostSerializer(serializers.ModelSerializer):
    class Meta:
```

153

```
model = BlogPost
fields = '__all__'  # Include all fields
```

Step 3: Implement CRUD API Views Using FBVs

Modify views.py:

python
CopyEdit
```python
from rest_framework.decorators import api_view
from rest_framework.response import Response
from rest_framework import status
from .models import BlogPost
from .serializers import BlogPostSerializer

@api_view(['GET', 'POST'])
def blog_list(request):
    if request.method == 'GET':
        posts = BlogPost.objects.all()
        serializer = BlogPostSerializer(posts, many=True)
        return Response(serializer.data)

    elif request.method == 'POST':
        serializer = BlogPostSerializer(data=request.data)
        if serializer.is_valid():
            serializer.save()
            return Response(serializer.data, status=status.HTTP_201_CREATED)
        return Response(serializer.errors, status=status.HTTP_400_BAD_REQUEST)

@api_view(['GET', 'PUT', 'DELETE'])
def blog_detail(request, pk):
    try:
        post = BlogPost.objects.get(pk=pk)
    except BlogPost.DoesNotExist:
        return Response({"error": "Not found"}, status=status.HTTP_404_NOT_FOUND)

    if request.method == 'GET':
        serializer = BlogPostSerializer(post)
        return Response(serializer.data)
```

```
elif request.method == 'PUT':
    serializer = BlogPostSerializer(post, data=request.data)
    if serializer.is_valid():
        serializer.save()
        return Response(serializer.data)
    return Response(serializer.errors, status=status.HTTP_400_BAD_REQUEST)

elif request.method == 'DELETE':
    post.delete()
    return Response(status=status.HTTP_204_NO_CONTENT)
```

Step 4: Map API Views to URLs (urls.py)

python
CopyEdit
```
urlpatterns += [
    path('api/posts/', blog_list, name='blog_list'),
    path('api/posts/<int:pk>/', blog_detail, name='blog_detail'),
]
```

Now, our API supports:

- GET /api/posts/ → Fetch all posts
- POST /api/posts/ → Create a new post
- GET /api/posts/<id>/ → Fetch a specific post
- PUT /api/posts/<id>/ → Update a post
- DELETE /api/posts/<id>/ → Delete a post

2.3 Class-Based API Views (CBVs)

CBVs use Django's **class-based view structure**, making them more **structured and reusable**.

155

Step 1: Implement CRUD API Using CBVs

Modify views.py:

python
CopyEdit
```python
from rest_framework import generics
from .models import BlogPost
from .serializers import BlogPostSerializer

class BlogListCreateView(generics.ListCreateAPIView):
    queryset = BlogPost.objects.all()
    serializer_class = BlogPostSerializer

class BlogDetailView(generics.RetrieveUpdateDestroyAPIView):
    queryset = BlogPost.objects.all()
    serializer_class = BlogPostSerializer
```

Step 2: Map CBVs to URLs

Modify urls.py:

python
CopyEdit
```python
urlpatterns += [
    path('api/cbv/posts/', BlogListCreateView.as_view(), name='blog_list_cbv'),
    path('api/cbv/posts/<int:pk>/', BlogDetailView.as_view(), name='blog_detail_cbv'),
]
```

Now, these CBVs provide the same CRUD functionality as FBVs but with **less code**.

2.4 FBVs vs. CBVs: Which One to Use?

Feature	Function-Based Views (FBVs)	Class-Based Views (CBVs)
Code Length	More lines required	Less code, DRY
Readability	Simple and explicit	More structured
Customization	More flexible	Uses DRF's built-in logic
Use Case	Small APIs, quick development	Large APIs, maintainability

For **small APIs**, FBVs are good for quick development. For **scalable applications**, CBVs provide **better reusability and structure**.

Using Django Serializers (ModelSerializer vs. Custom Serializers)

1.1 What Are Serializers?

Serializers in DRF work similarly to Django Forms but are used to **convert Python objects to JSON and vice versa**. They handle **data validation, parsing, and formatting**.

1.2 ModelSerializer: Simplifying Serialization

ModelSerializer **automatically** generates serializer fields from a Django model.

Example: Using ModelSerializer

Modify serializers.py:

python

CopyEdit

```
from rest_framework import serializers
from .models import BlogPost


class BlogPostSerializer(serializers.ModelSerializer):
    class Meta:
```

157

```python
    model = BlogPost

    fields = '__all__'  # Includes all model fields
```

- ModelSerializer **auto-generates fields** based on BlogPost model.
- Reduces boilerplate code compared to **custom serializers**.

1.3 Custom Serializers for More Control

Custom serializers provide **manual field definitions** and additional **validation logic**.

Example: Custom Serializer for BlogPost

python

CopyEdit

```python
class CustomBlogPostSerializer(serializers.Serializer):

    title = serializers.CharField(max_length=255)

    content = serializers.CharField()

    author = serializers.CharField(max_length=100)


    def create(self, validated_data):

        return BlogPost.objects.create(**validated_data)


    def update(self, instance, validated_data):

        instance.title = validated_data.get('title', instance.title)

        instance.content = validated_data.get('content', instance.content)

        instance.author = validated_data.get('author', instance.author)
```

158

```
instance.save()

return instance
```

- Requires **manual field definitions**.
- Must implement **create() and update()** methods.

1.4 Adding Custom Validation in Serializers

Example: Preventing Short Titles

python

CopyEdit

```python
class BlogPostSerializer(serializers.ModelSerializer):
    class Meta:
        model = BlogPost
        fields = '__all__'

    def validate_title(self, value):
        if len(value) < 5:
            raise serializers.ValidationError("Title must be at least 5 characters long.")
        return value
```

Now, if a user submits a **short title**, DRF returns a **validation error**.

1.5 ModelSerializer vs. Custom Serializer: When to Use?

Feature	ModelSerializer	Custom Serializer
Code Length	Less code	More manual work
Flexibility	Auto-generates fields	Full control
Use Case	Standard CRUD APIs	Custom business logic

■ Use ModelSerializer for **CRUD APIs**.
■ Use **custom serializers** for **complex data processing**.

Authentication for APIs: Token-Based, JWT, OAuth

APIs require authentication to ensure **secure access**. DRF supports multiple authentication mechanisms, including **Token-Based Authentication, JSON Web Tokens (JWT), and OAuth**.

2.1 Token-Based Authentication

Token authentication is **simpler than session-based authentication** and is commonly used for mobile apps and APIs.

Step 1: Enable Token Authentication in settings.py

python

CopyEdit

```
INSTALLED_APPS += ['rest_framework.authtoken']


REST_FRAMEWORK['DEFAULT_AUTHENTICATION_CLASSES'] = [

    'rest_framework.authentication.TokenAuthentication',

]
```

Step 2: Run Migrations for Token Model

sh

CopyEdit

```
python manage.py migrate
```

Step 3: Create API Views for Token Authentication

Modify views.py:

python

CopyEdit

```
from rest_framework.authtoken.models import Token
from rest_framework.decorators import api_view
from rest_framework.response import Response
from django.contrib.auth.models import User
from django.contrib.auth import authenticate


@api_view(['POST'])
def login_view(request):
    username = request.data.get('username')
    password = request.data.get('password')
    user = authenticate(username=username, password=password)
```

161

```python
if user:

    token, created = Token.objects.get_or_create(user=user)

    return Response({'token': token.key})

return Response({'error': 'Invalid credentials'}, status=400)
```

Step 4: Add API URL for Token Login

Modify urls.py:

python

CopyEdit

```python
from django.urls import path

from .views import login_view


urlpatterns = [

    path('api/token/login/', login_view, name='token_login'),

]
```

Step 5: Making API Requests with Tokens

Clients must **send the token** in the Authorization header:

sh

CopyEdit

```sh
curl -X GET http://127.0.0.1:8000/api/posts/ -H "Authorization: Token YOUR_TOKEN_HERE"
```

Now, only **authenticated users** can access the API.

2.2 JSON Web Token (JWT) Authentication

JWT authentication provides **stateless authentication** with signed tokens.

Step 1: Install Django REST Framework SimpleJWT

sh

CopyEdit

```
pip install djangorestframework-simplejwt
```

Step 2: Configure JWT in settings.py

python

CopyEdit

```
from datetime import timedelta


REST_FRAMEWORK['DEFAULT_AUTHENTICATION_CLASSES'] = [
    'rest_framework_simplejwt.authentication.JWTAuthentication',
]


SIMPLE_JWT = {
    'ACCESS_TOKEN_LIFETIME': timedelta(days=1),
    'REFRESH_TOKEN_LIFETIME': timedelta(days=7),
}
```

163

Step 3: Add JWT Authentication URLs

Modify urls.py:

python

CopyEdit

```
from rest_framework_simplejwt.views import TokenObtainPairView,
TokenRefreshView


urlpatterns += [

    path('api/token/', TokenObtainPairView.as_view(), name='token_obtain_pair'),

    path('api/token/refresh/', TokenRefreshView.as_view(), name='token_refresh'),

]
```

- api/token/ → **Generates an access and refresh token.**
- api/token/refresh/ → **Renews expired access tokens.**

Step 4: Making API Requests with JWT

1. **Obtain a JWT Token:**

sh

CopyEdit

```
curl -X POST http://127.0.0.1:8000/api/token/ -d
"username=john_doe&password=securepassword"
```

Response:

json

CopyEdit

```json
{
  "access": "ACCESS_TOKEN",
  "refresh": "REFRESH_TOKEN"
}
```

2. **Use the Access Token in Requests**:

sh

CopyEdit

```sh
curl -X GET http://127.0.0.1:8000/api/posts/ -H "Authorization: Bearer ACCESS_TOKEN"
```

Now, users can authenticate with **JWT tokens** instead of session-based logins.

2.3 OAuth Authentication with django-allauth

OAuth authentication allows users to **log in via third-party providers** like Google, Facebook, and GitHub.

Step 1: Install django-allauth

sh

CopyEdit

```sh
pip install django-allauth
```

Step 2: Configure OAuth in settings.py

Add **Google, Facebook, and GitHub authentication**:

python

CopyEdit

```
INSTALLED_APPS += [

    'allauth',

    'allauth.account',

    'allauth.socialaccount',

    'allauth.socialaccount.providers.google',

    'allauth.socialaccount.providers.github',

    'allauth.socialaccount.providers.facebook',

]
```

Set authentication backend:

python

CopyEdit

```
AUTHENTICATION_BACKENDS = [

    'django.contrib.auth.backends.ModelBackend',

    'allauth.account.auth_backends.AuthenticationBackend',

]
```

Step 3: Add OAuth URLs

Modify urls.py:

python

CopyEdit

```python
urlpatterns += [

    path('accounts/', include('allauth.urls')),

]
```

Users can now **log in via Google, GitHub, or Facebook.**

Implementing API Permissions and Rate Limiting

Permissions determine **who can access specific API endpoints**. DRF provides multiple levels of permission control:

- **Global Permissions** – Applied to all API views.
- **View-Level Permissions** – Set on a per-view basis.
- **Object-Level Permissions** – Grant access based on specific database objects.

1.1 Setting Up API Permissions

Modify settings.py to define **default permissions**:

python

CopyEdit

```python
REST_FRAMEWORK = {

    'DEFAULT_PERMISSION_CLASSES': [
```

'rest_framework.permissions.IsAuthenticated', # Only authenticated users can access APIs

```
    ]

}
```

Now, API access requires **user authentication**.

1.2 Using Built-in Permission Classes

DRF provides the following **predefined permission classes**:

Permission Class	Description
AllowAny	Public access (no restrictions).
IsAuthenticated	Only logged-in users can access.
IsAdminUser	Only staff/admin users can access.
IsAuthenticatedOrReadOnly	Authenticated users get full access; others can only read data.
DjangoModelPermissions	Uses Django model-level permissions.

1.3 Applying Permissions to API Views

You can set **permissions per view** using the permission_classes attribute.

Example: Restricting API Access to Authenticated Users Only

Modify views.py:

python

CopyEdit

```
from rest_framework.permissions import IsAuthenticated

from rest_framework import generics

from .models import BlogPost
```

```python
from .serializers import BlogPostSerializer


class BlogListCreateView(generics.ListCreateAPIView):

    queryset = BlogPost.objects.all()

    serializer_class = BlogPostSerializer

    permission_classes = [IsAuthenticated]  # Restrict access to authenticated users
```

Now, only **authenticated users** can create or retrieve blog posts.

1.4 Implementing Custom Permissions

Custom permissions allow defining **more granular access control**.

Example: Only Post Authors Can Edit/Delete Their Own Posts

Create a custom permission in permissions.py:

python

CopyEdit

```python
from rest_framework import permissions


class IsAuthorOrReadOnly(permissions.BasePermission):

    def has_object_permission(self, request, view, obj):

        # Read-only permissions are allowed for any request

        if request.method in permissions.SAFE_METHODS:

            return True
```

```
    # Write permissions are only allowed for the author of the post

    return obj.author == request.user
```

Apply it to views:

python

CopyEdit

```python
class BlogDetailView(generics.RetrieveUpdateDestroyAPIView):

    queryset = BlogPost.objects.all()

    serializer_class = BlogPostSerializer

    permission_classes = [IsAuthorOrReadOnly]
```

Now, only **post authors can edit or delete their own posts**, while others have **read-only access**.

1.5 Rate Limiting API Requests

Rate limiting prevents **abuse and excessive API calls**.

Step 1: Configure Rate Limiting in settings.py

python

CopyEdit

```python
REST_FRAMEWORK['DEFAULT_THROTTLE_CLASSES'] = [

    'rest_framework.throttling.UserRateThrottle',

    'rest_framework.throttling.AnonRateThrottle',

]
```

170

```
REST_FRAMEWORK['DEFAULT_THROTTLE_RATES'] = {
    'user': '10/minute',  # Authenticated users can make 10 requests per minute
    'anon': '5/minute',  # Anonymous users can make 5 requests per minute
}
```

Step 2: Apply Rate Limits to API Views

Modify views.py:

python

CopyEdit

```
from rest_framework.throttling import UserRateThrottle
from rest_framework.permissions import IsAuthenticated


class BlogListCreateView(generics.ListCreateAPIView):
    queryset = BlogPost.objects.all()
    serializer_class = BlogPostSerializer
    permission_classes = [IsAuthenticated]
    throttle_classes = [UserRateThrottle]  # Apply rate limiting
```

If a user **exceeds their allowed requests**, DRF returns:

json

CopyEdit

```
{

    "detail": "Request was throttled. Expected available in X seconds."

}
```

Building a Full API: CRUD Operations with Django REST Framework

A fully functional API should **support all CRUD operations** for managing resources.

2.1 Define the Model (models.py)

python

CopyEdit

```
from django.db import models

from django.contrib.auth.models import User


class BlogPost(models.Model):

    title = models.CharField(max_length=255)

    content = models.TextField()

    author = models.ForeignKey(User, on_delete=models.CASCADE)

    created_at = models.DateTimeField(auto_now_add=True)
```

2.2 Create a Serializer (serializers.py)

python

CopyEdit

```python
from rest_framework import serializers
from .models import BlogPost


class BlogPostSerializer(serializers.ModelSerializer):
    class Meta:
        model = BlogPost
        fields = '__all__'
```

2.3 Implement API Views (views.py)

1. List and Create Blog Posts (GET, POST)

python

CopyEdit

```python
from rest_framework import generics
from .models import BlogPost
from .serializers import BlogPostSerializer
from rest_framework.permissions import IsAuthenticated


class BlogListCreateView(generics.ListCreateAPIView):
    queryset = BlogPost.objects.all()
```

173

```python
serializer_class = BlogPostSerializer

permission_classes = [IsAuthenticated]
```

- GET /api/posts/ – **Retrieves all blog posts.**
- POST /api/posts/ – **Creates a new blog post.**

2. Retrieve, Update, and Delete Blog Posts (GET, PUT, DELETE)

python

CopyEdit

```python
class BlogDetailView(generics.RetrieveUpdateDestroyAPIView):

    queryset = BlogPost.objects.all()

    serializer_class = BlogPostSerializer

    permission_classes = [IsAuthenticated]
```

- GET /api/posts/<id>/ – **Fetches a single post.**
- PUT /api/posts/<id>/ – **Updates a post.**
- DELETE /api/posts/<id>/ – **Deletes a post.**

2.4 Set Up API URLs (urls.py)

python

CopyEdit

```python
from django.urls import path

from .views import BlogListCreateView, BlogDetailView
```

174

```
urlpatterns = [

    path('api/posts/', BlogListCreateView.as_view(), name='blog_list'),

    path('api/posts/<int:pk>/', BlogDetailView.as_view(), name='blog_detail'),

]
```

2.5 Testing API Endpoints

1. Creating a Blog Post (POST Request)

sh

CopyEdit

```
curl -X POST http://127.0.0.1:8000/api/posts/ -H "Authorization: Bearer ACCESS_TOKEN" -d "title=My First Post&content=Hello World&author=1"
```

2. Fetching All Blog Posts (GET Request)

sh

CopyEdit

```
curl -X GET http://127.0.0.1:8000/api/posts/ -H "Authorization: Bearer ACCESS_TOKEN"
```

3. Updating a Post (PUT Request)

sh

CopyEdit

```
curl -X PUT http://127.0.0.1:8000/api/posts/1/ -H "Authorization: Bearer ACCESS_TOKEN" -d "title=Updated Title"
```

4. Deleting a Post (DELETE Request)

sh

CopyEdit

curl -X DELETE http://127.0.0.1:8000/api/posts/1/ -H "Authorization: Bearer ACCESS_TOKEN"

Now, our API is fully functional!

Key Takeaways

■ **Permissions Restrict API Access** – Use IsAuthenticated, IsAdminUser, and custom permissions.
■ **Rate Limiting Prevents API Abuse** – Apply request throttling using DRF's throttling classes.
■ **CRUD Operations Manage API Resources** – Implement Create, Read, Update, and Delete endpoints.
■ **DRF Simplifies API Development** – ModelSerializer, APIView, and generics provide flexible API structures.

Chapter 8: Asynchronous Django & Real-Time Applications

As web applications evolve, real-time features like **live notifications, chat applications, and live updates** have become essential. Django traditionally operates in a **synchronous (blocking) request-response cycle**, but with the introduction of **async support in Django** and **Django Channels**, developers can now build fully **asynchronous, event-driven applications**.

Understanding Django's Asynchronous Features

Django initially relied entirely on **synchronous execution** with WSGI (Web Server Gateway Interface). However, modern applications need to handle **concurrent requests, long-running tasks, and real-time updates**. With the introduction of **ASGI (Asynchronous Server Gateway Interface)**, Django now supports **asynchronous views, database queries, and WebSockets**.

1.1 How Does Asynchronous Django Work?

Django's async support is built around **Python's asyncio framework**. This allows Django to:

- Handle **multiple requests concurrently**.
- Use **async database queries** for non-blocking database operations.
- Implement **WebSockets for real-time communication**.

Django 3.1 introduced **partial async support**, while Django 4.x expanded it to include:
- **Asynchronous views**
- **Async ORM queries (Django 4.1+)**
- **Integration with Django Channels for WebSockets**

1.2 Writing Asynchronous Django Views

Django now supports **async views**, which allow handling **non-blocking** operations.

Example: Sync vs. Async View

Modify views.py:

python
CopyEdit
```python
from django.http import JsonResponse
import asyncio

# Synchronous View (Blocks Execution)
def sync_view(request):
    import time
    time.sleep(5)  # Simulates a long-running process
    return JsonResponse({"message": "This is a sync response!"})

# Asynchronous View (Non-blocking)
async def async_view(request):
    await asyncio.sleep(5)  # Non-blocking wait
    return JsonResponse({"message": "This is an async response!"})
```

Mapping Views in urls.py

python
CopyEdit
```python
from django.urls import path
from .views import sync_view, async_view

urlpatterns = [
    path('sync/', sync_view, name='sync_view'),
    path('async/', async_view, name='async_view'),
]
```

■ The **sync view blocks execution** for 5 seconds.
■ The **async view** allows **other requests to be processed concurrently**.

1.3 Running Django with ASGI

Django uses **ASGI (Asynchronous Server Gateway Interface)** to handle async views, WebSockets, and background tasks.

Step 1: Update asgi.py

Modify asgi.py in your Django project:

```python
CopyEdit
import os
from django.core.asgi import get_asgi_application

os.environ.setdefault('DJANGO_SETTINGS_MODULE', 'myproject.settings')

application = get_asgi_application()
```

Now, Django is running with **ASGI**, allowing **async execution**.

1.4 Asynchronous Database Queries

Django 4.1 introduced **async ORM queries**, allowing developers to run non-blocking queries.

Example: Running Async Queries

```python
CopyEdit
from django.http import JsonResponse
from .models import BlogPost

async def async_db_query(request):
    posts = await BlogPost.objects.all()  # Async ORM query
    data = [{"title": post.title, "content": post.content} for post in posts]
    return JsonResponse(data, safe=False)
```

Now, database queries run **without blocking other requests**.

Using Django Channels for WebSockets

Django Channels extends Django's capabilities by enabling **WebSockets, background tasks, and real-time event handling**.

2.1 What Are WebSockets?

Unlike HTTP, which follows a **request-response** cycle, **WebSockets** provide a **persistent connection** between the server and the client, allowing **bi-directional communication in real-time**.

■ Ideal for **chat applications, notifications, live tracking, and collaborative apps**.
■ Reduces **network overhead** compared to polling-based approaches.

2.2 Installing and Configuring Django Channels

Install Django Channels:

```sh
CopyEdit
pip install channels
```

Add it to INSTALLED_APPS in settings.py:

```python
CopyEdit
INSTALLED_APPS = [
    'channels',
    'myapp',  # Your Django app
]
```

Modify asgi.py to use **Django Channels**:

```python
CopyEdit
import os
```

```python
from django.core.asgi import get_asgi_application
from channels.routing import ProtocolTypeRouter, URLRouter
from myapp.routing import websocket_urlpatterns

os.environ.setdefault('DJANGO_SETTINGS_MODULE', 'myproject.settings')

application = ProtocolTypeRouter({
    "http": get_asgi_application(),  # Standard HTTP handling
    "websocket": URLRouter(websocket_urlpatterns),  # WebSocket handling
})
```

Now, Django can handle **both HTTP requests and WebSockets**.

2.3 Creating a WebSocket Consumer

Consumers in Django Channels handle **WebSocket events**, similar to Django views.

Step 1: Define a WebSocket Consumer

Create consumers.py in your Django app:

python
CopyEdit
```python
import json
from channels.generic.websocket import AsyncWebsocketConsumer

class ChatConsumer(AsyncWebsocketConsumer):
    async def connect(self):
        await self.accept()  # Accept WebSocket connection
        await self.send(text_data=json.dumps({"message": "WebSocket connected!"}))

    async def disconnect(self, close_code):
        print("WebSocket disconnected")

    async def receive(self, text_data):
        data = json.loads(text_data)
        message = data.get("message", "")
```

```
# Send response to WebSocket client
await self.send(text_data=json.dumps({"response": f"You said: {message}"}))
```

- connect() → Handles new WebSocket connections.
- disconnect() → Handles disconnections.
- receive() → Handles incoming messages.

2.4 Mapping WebSocket URLs

Create a new routing.py file inside your app:

python
CopyEdit
```
from django.urls import re_path
from .consumers import ChatConsumer

websocket_urlpatterns = [
    re_path(r'ws/chat/$', ChatConsumer.as_asgi()),  # WebSocket endpoint
]
```

Now, WebSockets are accessible at **ws://localhost:8000/ws/chat/**.

2.5 Running Django with WebSockets

Start the Django development server:

sh
CopyEdit
```
python manage.py runserver
```

Now, WebSockets are active.

182

2.6 Testing WebSockets with JavaScript

Modify chat.html:

html
CopyEdit

```html
<script>
  let socket = new WebSocket("ws://localhost:8000/ws/chat/");

  socket.onmessage = function(event) {
    let data = JSON.parse(event.data);
    console.log("Message from server:", data.message);
  };

  function sendMessage() {
    let message = document.getElementById("message").value;
    socket.send(JSON.stringify({ "message": message }));
  }
</script>

<input type="text" id="message">
<button onclick="sendMessage()">Send</button>
```

■ Open the browser console to see WebSocket messages in real-time.

2.7 Broadcasting Messages to Multiple Clients

Modify ChatConsumer to **broadcast messages** to multiple users:

python
CopyEdit

```python
from channels.layers import get_channel_layer
from asgiref.sync import async_to_sync

class ChatConsumer(AsyncWebsocketConsumer):
    async def connect(self):
        self.room_name = "global_chat"
```

183

```python
        self.room_group_name = f"chat_{self.room_name}"

        await self.channel_layer.group_add(self.room_group_name, self.channel_name)
        await self.accept()

    async def receive(self, text_data):
        data = json.loads(text_data)
        message = data.get("message", "")

        await self.channel_layer.group_send(
            self.room_group_name, {"type": "chat_message", "message": message}
        )

    async def chat_message(self, event):
        await self.send(text_data=json.dumps({"message": event["message"]}))
```

Now, multiple users **receive messages in real-time**.

Building a Real-Time Chat App with Django Channels

A **chat application** requires the ability to:
■ Handle **multiple concurrent users**.
■ Allow users to **send and receive messages instantly**.
■ Store **chat messages in a database** for persistence.

1.1 Install and Configure Django Channels

Step 1: Install Django Channels
sh
CopyEdit
pip install channels

Step 2: Add Channels to INSTALLED_APPS

Modify settings.py:

python
CopyEdit
```
INSTALLED_APPS += [
    'channels',
    'chat',  # Chat app
]
```

Step 3: Update ASGI Configuration

Modify asgi.py to use Django Channels:

python
CopyEdit
```
import os
from django.core.asgi import get_asgi_application
from channels.routing import ProtocolTypeRouter, URLRouter
from chat.routing import websocket_urlpatterns

os.environ.setdefault('DJANGO_SETTINGS_MODULE', 'myproject.settings')

application = ProtocolTypeRouter({
    "http": get_asgi_application(),
    "websocket": URLRouter(websocket_urlpatterns),  # WebSocket support
})
```

Now, Django supports **WebSockets**.

185

1.2 Creating WebSocket Consumers for Chat

Step 1: Define a WebSocket Consumer

Create consumers.py in the chat app:

python
CopyEdit

```python
import json
from channels.generic.websocket import AsyncWebsocketConsumer

class ChatConsumer(AsyncWebsocketConsumer):
    async def connect(self):
        self.room_group_name = "chat_room"
        await self.channel_layer.group_add(self.room_group_name, self.channel_name)
        await self.accept()

    async def disconnect(self, close_code):
        await self.channel_layer.group_discard(self.room_group_name, self.channel_name)

    async def receive(self, text_data):
        data = json.loads(text_data)
        message = data.get("message", "")

        # Broadcast message to all connected clients
        await self.channel_layer.group_send(
            self.room_group_name, {"type": "chat_message", "message": message}
        )

    async def chat_message(self, event):
        await self.send(text_data=json.dumps({"message": event["message"]}))
```

■ **WebSocket Lifecycle:**

- connect() → User **joins** the chat.
- disconnect() → User **leaves** the chat.
- receive() → Handles **incoming messages**.
- chat_message() → Sends messages to **all connected users**.

186

Step 2: Define WebSocket Routing

Create routing.py inside the chat app:

python
CopyEdit
```python
from django.urls import re_path
from .consumers import ChatConsumer

websocket_urlpatterns = [
    re_path(r'ws/chat/$', ChatConsumer.as_asgi()),
]
```

1.3 Creating the Chat Room UI

Modify chat.html:

html
CopyEdit
```html
<!DOCTYPE html>
<html>
<head>
    <title>Chat Room</title>
</head>
<body>
    <h2>Real-Time Chat</h2>
    <textarea id="chat-log" cols="50" rows="10" readonly></textarea><br>
    <input id="chat-message" type="text">
    <button onclick="sendMessage()">Send</button>

    <script>
        let socket = new WebSocket("ws://localhost:8000/ws/chat/");

        socket.onmessage = function(event) {
            let data = JSON.parse(event.data);
            document.getElementById("chat-log").value += data.message + "\n";
        };
```

```
function sendMessage() {
    let message = document.getElementById("chat-message").value;
    socket.send(JSON.stringify({ "message": message }));
    }
</script>
</body>
</html>
```

Now, users can **send and receive messages in real time**!

Background Tasks with Celery and Redis

Long-running tasks, such as **sending emails, processing images, and fetching data from APIs**, should not block the main Django process. **Celery** is an asynchronous task queue that works with **Redis** to process jobs in the background.

2.1 Installing and Configuring Celery

Step 1: Install Celery and Redis
sh
CopyEdit
```
pip install celery redis
```

Ensure Redis is running:

sh
CopyEdit
```
sudo systemctl start redis
```

Step 2: Configure Celery in Django

Create a celery.py file inside your Django project:

python
CopyEdit
```python
import os
from celery import Celery

os.environ.setdefault('DJANGO_SETTINGS_MODULE', 'myproject.settings')

celery_app = Celery('myproject')
celery_app.config_from_object('django.conf:settings', namespace='CELERY')
celery_app.autodiscover_tasks()
```

Modify settings.py:

python
CopyEdit
```python
CELERY_BROKER_URL = 'redis://localhost:6379/0'
CELERY_ACCEPT_CONTENT = ['json']
CELERY_TASK_SERIALIZER = 'json'
```

2.2 Creating Celery Tasks

Step 1: Create a Background Task

Inside tasks.py in your app:

python
CopyEdit
```python
from celery import shared_task
from time import sleep

@shared_task
def send_email_notification(user_email):
    sleep(5)  # Simulates email sending delay
    return f"Email sent to {user_email}"
```

189

Step 2: Calling a Celery Task from Views

Modify views.py:

python
CopyEdit
```
from django.http import JsonResponse
from .tasks import send_email_notification

def trigger_email(request):
    user_email = request.GET.get('email', 'test@example.com')
    send_email_notification.delay(user_email)  # Call task asynchronously
    return JsonResponse({"message": "Email processing started!"})
```

Step 3: Running Celery Workers

Start Celery with:

sh
CopyEdit
```
celery -A myproject worker --loglevel=info
```

Celery now listens for background tasks and **executes them asynchronously**.

2.3 Periodic Tasks with Celery Beat

Celery can schedule **recurring tasks** using **Celery Beat**.

Step 1: Install Celery Beat
sh
CopyEdit
```
pip install django-celery-beat
```

Add it to INSTALLED_APPS:

python
CopyEdit
```
INSTALLED_APPS += ['django_celery_beat']
```

Run migrations:

sh
CopyEdit
```
python manage.py migrate django_celery_beat
```

Step 2: Configure Celery Beat in settings.py

python
CopyEdit
```
CELERY_BEAT_SCHEDULE = {
    'send_reminders': {
        'task': 'myapp.tasks.send_email_notification',
        'schedule': 60.0,  # Runs every 60 seconds
        'args': ("test@example.com",)
    },
}
```

Step 3: Running Celery Beat

Start Celery Beat:

sh
CopyEdit
```
celery -A myproject beat --loglevel=info
```

Now, Celery **automatically schedules tasks**.

Key Takeaways

■ **Django Channels Enables Real-Time WebSockets** – Build chat apps, live notifications, and real-time dashboards.
■ **Celery and Redis Handle Background Tasks** – Efficiently process emails, image processing, and API requests asynchronously.
■ **Celery Beat Automates Periodic Tasks** – Run scheduled jobs like email reminders, reports, and cache clearing.

With Django Channels, Celery, and Redis, developers can build **scalable real-time applications** that handle both **instant communication and background task execution efficiently**.

Chapter 9: Django Testing and Debugging

Building a **robust, bug-free** Django application requires **proper testing and debugging**. Django provides a **built-in testing framework** that allows developers to **write unit tests for models, views, and forms**, ensuring that the application behaves as expected.

Writing Unit Tests for Models, Views, and Forms

Unit tests help verify **individual components** of a Django application.

- **Model tests** ensure database integrity.
- **View tests** confirm correct HTTP responses.
- **Form tests** validate form behavior and data validation.

1.1 Setting Up Django's Test Environment

Django's test system is based on Python's unittest module. Tests should be placed inside a tests.py **file** in each Django app.

Ensure TEST_RUNNER is enabled in settings.py (enabled by default):

```python
CopyEdit
TEST_RUNNER = 'django.test.runner.DiscoverRunner'
```

To run tests:

```sh
CopyEdit
python manage.py test
```

Django automatically **creates a temporary test database** and resets data after tests are complete.

1.2 Writing Unit Tests for Django Models

Model tests ensure that **database models function correctly**.

Example: Testing a BlogPost Model

Modify models.py:

python
CopyEdit
```python
from django.db import models

class BlogPost(models.Model):
    title = models.CharField(max_length=255)
    content = models.TextField()
    created_at = models.DateTimeField(auto_now_add=True)
```

Now, create a **test file** (tests.py) inside the app directory:

python
CopyEdit
```python
from django.test import TestCase
from .models import BlogPost

class BlogPostModelTest(TestCase):
    def setUp(self):
        self.blog = BlogPost.objects.create(title="Test Title", content="Test content.")

    def test_blog_creation(self):
        """Test if the blog post is created correctly"""
        self.assertEqual(self.blog.title, "Test Title")
        self.assertEqual(self.blog.content, "Test content.")

    def test_blog_str_method(self):
        """Test the __str__ method"""
        self.assertEqual(str(self.blog), "Test Title")
```

- setUp() creates a sample blog post.
- test_blog_creation() ensures **correct field values**.
- test_blog_str_method() verifies **string representation**.

1.3 Writing Unit Tests for Django Views

View tests ensure that **API responses and page rendering** work correctly.

Example: Testing a Blog List View

Modify views.py:

python
CopyEdit
```python
from django.http import JsonResponse
from .models import BlogPost

def blog_list(request):
    posts = list(BlogPost.objects.values("title", "content"))
    return JsonResponse({"posts": posts})
```

Now, test the view in tests.py:

python
CopyEdit
```python
from django.test import TestCase
from django.urls import reverse
from .models import BlogPost

class BlogPostViewTest(TestCase):
    def setUp(self):
        BlogPost.objects.create(title="Test Post", content="This is a test.")

    def test_blog_list_view(self):
        """Ensure the blog list view returns correct data"""
        response = self.client.get(reverse("blog_list"))
        self.assertEqual(response.status_code, 200)
        self.assertContains(response, "Test Post")
```

195

- self.client.get() simulates an **HTTP GET request**.
- reverse("blog_list") resolves the URL dynamically.
- assertContains() checks if the response **contains expected content**.

1.4 Writing Unit Tests for Django Forms

Form tests ensure **data validation works correctly**.

Modify forms.py:

python
CopyEdit
```python
from django import forms
from .models import BlogPost

class BlogPostForm(forms.ModelForm):
    class Meta:
        model = BlogPost
        fields = ['title', 'content']
```

Now, test the form in tests.py:

python
CopyEdit
```python
from django.test import TestCase
from .forms import BlogPostForm

class BlogPostFormTest(TestCase):
    def test_valid_form(self):
        """Check if the form is valid with correct data"""
        form_data = {"title": "Valid Title", "content": "Valid content."}
        form = BlogPostForm(data=form_data)
        self.assertTrue(form.is_valid())

    def test_invalid_form(self):
        """Ensure form fails when missing required fields"""
```

196

```
form_data = {"title": ""}
form = BlogPostForm(data=form_data)
self.assertFalse(form.is_valid())
```

- test_valid_form() checks if the form **accepts correct data**.
- test_invalid_form() verifies **form validation fails for missing fields**.

Using Django's Built-in Test Framework

Django provides a powerful testing framework built on Python's unittest.

2.1 Running Django Tests

To run all tests:

sh
CopyEdit
```
python manage.py test
```

To run tests for a specific app:

sh
CopyEdit
```
python manage.py test myapp
```

To run a **specific test case**:

sh
CopyEdit
```
python manage.py test myapp.tests.BlogPostViewTest
```

To run a **single test method**:

sh
CopyEdit
```
python manage.py test myapp.tests.BlogPostViewTest.test_blog_list_view
```
197

2.2 Using Django's Test Client for HTTP Requests

Django's self.client simulates a web browser for testing views.

Example: Simulating a User Login Test
python
CopyEdit
```
from django.contrib.auth.models import User
from django.test import TestCase

class UserLoginTest(TestCase):
    def setUp(self):
        self.user = User.objects.create_user(username="testuser", password="testpass")

    def test_login(self):
        """Test user login with valid credentials"""
        response = self.client.post("/login/", {"username": "testuser", "password": "testpass"})
        self.assertEqual(response.status_code, 200)
```

■ self.client.post() simulates **form submission** for login.
■ assertEqual(response.status_code, 200) ensures **successful login**.

2.3 Using Django's Test Database

Django automatically creates a **test database** for tests.

- **Test database is created before tests run.**
- **Database is deleted after tests complete.**
- **Modifications to test data don't affect the real database.**

Example:

python
CopyEdit
```
from django.test import TestCase
from .models import BlogPost
```

```python
class TestDatabase(TestCase):
    def test_create_blog(self):
        """Test creating a blog post in the test database"""
        post = BlogPost.objects.create(title="Test Post", content="Some content.")
        self.assertEqual(BlogPost.objects.count(), 1)
```

Even though we create a blog post, it **won't persist in the real database**.

2.4 Mocking External API Calls in Django Tests

If your Django app interacts with external APIs, you can **mock API responses**.

Example: Mocking an External API Request

Modify views.py:

python
CopyEdit
```python
import requests
from django.http import JsonResponse

def fetch_api_data(request):
    response = requests.get("https://api.example.com/data")
    return JsonResponse(response.json())
```

Now, mock the API in tests.py:

python
CopyEdit
```python
from django.test import TestCase
from unittest.mock import patch
import requests

class APITest(TestCase):
    @patch("requests.get")
    def test_mock_api(self, mock_get):
        """Mock an external API response"""
```

199

```
mock_get.return_value.json.return_value = {"data": "mock response"}

response = self.client.get("/api/data/")
self.assertEqual(response.json(), {"data": "mock response"})
```

■ @patch("requests.get") replaces the real API call with a **mocked response**.
■ Tests **run faster** without making real network requests.

Debugging Django Apps with Django Debug Toolbar

Django Debug Toolbar is a **real-time debugging tool** that provides insights into:
■ **SQL queries** – Detecting slow or excessive database queries.
■ **Request/response cycles** – Measuring the time taken for HTTP requests.
■ **Cache usage** – Identifying inefficient caching.
■ **Template rendering** – Understanding how long it takes to process templates.

1.1 Installing Django Debug Toolbar

Run the installation command:

sh

CopyEdit

```
pip install django-debug-toolbar
```


1.2 Configuring Django Debug Toolbar

Step 1: Add Debug Toolbar to Installed Apps

Modify settings.py:

python

CopyEdit

```
INSTALLED_APPS += ['debug_toolbar']
```

200

Step 2: Add Debug Toolbar Middleware

Modify MIDDLEWARE in settings.py:

python

CopyEdit

```
MIDDLEWARE += ['debug_toolbar.middleware.DebugToolbarMiddleware']
```

Step 3: Configure Internal IPs for Local Development

Add the following to settings.py:

python

CopyEdit

```
INTERNAL_IPS = [
    "127.0.0.1",
]
```

1.3 Adding Debug Toolbar to Django URLs

Modify urls.py:

python

CopyEdit

```
from django.conf import settings
from django.conf.urls import include
from django.urls import path
```

```
urlpatterns = [

    # Your other URLs here

]


if settings.DEBUG:

    import debug_toolbar

    urlpatterns += [path('__debug__/', include(debug_toolbar.urls))]
```

Now, Django Debug Toolbar is accessible at http://127.0.0.1:8000/__debug__/.

1.4 Using Django Debug Toolbar

Start the development server:

sh

CopyEdit

```
python manage.py runserver
```


Visit **any page in your Django app,** and you'll see a **collapsible toolbar** on the right-hand side of the screen. This toolbar provides:
- **Time taken for request processing**
- **Database queries executed per page**
- **Cache hits and misses**
- **Template rendering time**

1.5 Debugging Database Queries

Django Debug Toolbar helps identify **slow or redundant queries**.

Example:
If your page is running **too many queries**, you might see **N+1 query issues**, where Django runs an extra query for each object in a loop.

Bad Query (Causing N+1 Problem):

python

CopyEdit

```
posts = BlogPost.objects.all()

for post in posts:

    print(post.author.username)  # This triggers extra queries for each post
```

Optimized Query (Using select_related to reduce queries):

python

CopyEdit

```
posts = BlogPost.objects.select_related('author')
```

■ The Debug Toolbar will show **fewer queries** and **better performance**.

Profiling and Performance Optimization Techniques

Performance profiling helps identify **slow parts of an application**, such as **long-running database queries, slow views, or inefficient template rendering**.

2.1 Profiling Django Views with Silk

Silk is a **Django profiling tool** that provides **detailed performance analysis**.

Step 1: Install Silk

sh

CopyEdit

```
pip install django-silk
```

Step 2: Add Silk to Installed Apps

Modify settings.py:

python

CopyEdit

```
INSTALLED_APPS += ['silk']

MIDDLEWARE += ['silk.middleware.SilkyMiddleware']
```

Step 3: Run Migrations and Start Silk

sh

CopyEdit

```
python manage.py migrate silk
```

Step 4: Add Silk URLs

Modify urls.py:

python

CopyEdit

```
urlpatterns += [path('silk/', include('silk.urls', namespace='silk'))]
```

Now, visit http://127.0.0.1:8000/silk/ to view **profiling reports**.

2.2 Optimizing Database Queries

Django's ORM provides **several optimizations** for reducing query overhead.

Using select_related() for Foreign Keys

Instead of making **multiple queries** for related objects:

python

CopyEdit

```
# Bad Query - Causes Multiple Queries
posts = BlogPost.objects.all()
for post in posts:
    print(post.author.username)  # Extra query for each author
```

Use select_related() to optimize:

python

CopyEdit

```
# Optimized Query
posts = BlogPost.objects.select_related('author')
```

■ Reduces **extra queries**, making it **faster**.

Using prefetch_related() for Many-to-Many Relationships

Instead of fetching **related objects individually**:

python

CopyEdit

```
# Bad Query - Causes Multiple Queries
categories = Category.objects.all()
for category in categories:
    print(category.posts.all())  # Triggers extra queries
```

Use prefetch_related():

python

CopyEdit

```
# Optimized Query
categories = Category.objects.prefetch_related('posts')
```

■ Reduces **query duplication** for many-to-many relationships.

2.3 Caching for Performance Improvement

Caching reduces **unnecessary database hits** and speeds up page loads.

Step 1: Enable Caching in Django

Modify settings.py:

python

CopyEdit

```
CACHES = {
    'default': {
        'BACKEND': 'django.core.cache.backends.memcached.MemcachedCache',
        'LOCATION': '127.0.0.1:11211',
    }
}
```


Step 2: Cache Expensive Queries

Instead of fetching from the database **every time**:

python

CopyEdit

```
posts = BlogPost.objects.all()  # Query runs every time
```

Use caching:

python

CopyEdit

```
from django.core.cache import cache

posts = cache.get('blog_posts')
if not posts:
    posts = BlogPost.objects.all()
    cache.set('blog_posts', posts, timeout=60*15)  # Cache for 15 minutes
```

■ Reduces **database queries** and improves **performance**.

2.4 Optimizing Template Rendering

Django templates can be **optimized** by:

■ **Avoiding complex logic in templates**
■ **Using {% cache %} template tag**

Example:

html

CopyEdit

```
{% load cache %}
{% cache 300 post_list %}
    {% for post in posts %}
        <h2>{{ post.title }}</h2>
```

208

```
{% endfor %}

{% endcache %}
```

■ **Caches template rendering for 5 minutes (300 seconds).**

2.5 Lazy Loading vs. Eager Loading

Lazy Loading (default behavior) loads objects **only when accessed**, but it can cause **N+1 query issues**.
Eager Loading (select_related() and prefetch_related()) **reduces queries** and improves performance.

Example:

python

CopyEdit

```python
# Bad: Lazy Loading (Multiple Queries)

posts = BlogPost.objects.all()

for post in posts:

    print(post.author.username)  # Extra queries for each post
```

python

CopyEdit

```python
# Good: Eager Loading (Single Optimized Query)

posts = BlogPost.objects.select_related('author')
```

■ Reduces database **query load**.

2.6 Using Django QuerySet only() and defer()

If you don't need all fields, **avoid loading unnecessary data**.

python

CopyEdit

```python
# Load only specific fields
posts = BlogPost.objects.only('title', 'created_at')
```

python

CopyEdit

```python
# Defer loading large fields
posts = BlogPost.objects.defer('content')
```

■ Saves memory by **loading only required data**.

Chapter 10: Frontend Integration: Django with React, Vue.js, and HTMX

Modern web applications often rely on **frontend frameworks like React, Vue.js, and HTMX** to create dynamic user experiences. Django provides a powerful backend for handling **data, authentication, and business logic**, while frontend frameworks manage **interactive user interfaces**.

Serving Static Files and APIs to Frontend Frameworks

When integrating Django with a frontend framework like **React, Vue.js, or HTMX**, we need to:
■ Serve **static files (CSS, JavaScript, images)**.
■ Expose **Django REST APIs** for frontend applications.
■ Handle **CORS (Cross-Origin Resource Sharing)** to allow API requests from frontend apps.

1.1 Configuring Django to Serve Static Files

Django serves static files using the django.contrib.staticfiles app.

Step 1: Define Static File Settings

Modify settings.py:

```python
CopyEdit
import os

STATIC_URL = '/static/'
STATICFILES_DIRS = [os.path.join(BASE_DIR, 'static')]  # Development
STATIC_ROOT = os.path.join(BASE_DIR, 'staticfiles')  # Production
```

Step 2: Collect Static Files for Deployment

Run:

```sh
CopyEdit
python manage.py collectstatic
```
211

Django will gather all static files into the staticfiles/ directory.

1.2 Enabling CORS for API Requests from Frontend Apps

By default, Django REST APIs **reject cross-origin requests** from frontend frameworks. To allow React or Vue.js to access Django's API, install and configure **django-cors-headers**.

Step 1: Install CORS Headers
sh
CopyEdit
```
pip install django-cors-headers
```

Step 2: Configure Middleware in settings.py
python
CopyEdit
```
INSTALLED_APPS += ['corsheaders']

MIDDLEWARE += ['corsheaders.middleware.CorsMiddleware']

CORS_ALLOWED_ORIGINS = [
    "http://localhost:3000",  # React frontend
    "http://localhost:5173",  # Vue.js frontend
]
```

Now, Django will **allow API requests** from React (localhost:3000) or Vue.js (localhost:5173).

1.3 Exposing Django REST API for Frontend Apps

Django REST Framework (DRF) provides API endpoints that frontend frameworks can consume.

Example. Create an API to **list blog posts**.

Modify views.py:

python
CopyEdit
```python
from rest_framework.response import Response
from rest_framework.decorators import api_view
from .models import BlogPost
from .serializers import BlogPostSerializer

@api_view(['GET'])
def blog_list(request):
    posts = BlogPost.objects.all()
    serializer = BlogPostSerializer(posts, many=True)
    return Response(serializer.data)
```

Map the API in urls.py:

python
CopyEdit
```python
from django.urls import path
from .views import blog_list

urlpatterns = [
    path('api/posts/', blog_list, name='blog_list'),
]
```

Now, **React, Vue.js, or HTMX** can fetch data from /api/posts/.

Connecting Django REST Framework with React

React is a popular frontend library for building **dynamic user interfaces**. It communicates with Django REST APIs via **HTTP requests**.

213

2.1 Setting Up a React Frontend

Step 1: Create a React App

Navigate to your project directory and run:

```sh
CopyEdit
npx create-react-app myfrontend
cd myfrontend
```

Step 2: Install Axios for API Calls

Axios simplifies API requests:

```sh
CopyEdit
npm install axios
```

2.2 Fetching Data from Django API in React

Modify src/App.js:

```javascript
CopyEdit
import React, { useState, useEffect } from "react";
import axios from "axios";

const App = () => {
  const [posts, setPosts] = useState([]);

  useEffect(() => {
    axios.get("http://127.0.0.1:8000/api/posts/")
      .then(response => setPosts(response.data))
      .catch(error => console.error("Error fetching data:", error));
  }, []);

  return (
```

```
  <div>
    <h1>Blog Posts</h1>
    {posts.map(post => (
      <div key={post.id}>
        <h2>{post.title}</h2>
        <p>{post.content}</p>
      </div>
    ))}
  </div>
  );
};

export default App;
```

- **useEffect fetches data** when the component mounts.
- **axios.get("http://127.0.0.1:8000/api/posts/") requests Django's API**.
- **State (useState) updates dynamically** as data is fetched.

2.3 Handling Authentication in React with Django API

Django REST Framework (DRF) supports **JWT (JSON Web Token) authentication**, allowing React to securely authenticate users.

Step 1: Install JWT Authentication in Django
sh
CopyEdit
```
pip install djangorestframework-simplejwt
```

Modify settings.py:

python
CopyEdit
```
from datetime import timedelta

INSTALLED_APPS += ['rest_framework_simplejwt']
```

215

```
REST_FRAMEWORK['DEFAULT_AUTHENTICATION_CLASSES'] = [
    'rest_framework_simplejwt.authentication.JWTAuthentication',
]

SIMPLE_JWT = {
    'ACCESS_TOKEN_LIFETIME': timedelta(days=1),
}
```

Step 2: Create Login API in Django

Modify urls.py:

python
CopyEdit
```python
from rest_framework_simplejwt.views import TokenObtainPairView,
TokenRefreshView

urlpatterns += [
    path('api/token/', TokenObtainPairView.as_view(), name='token_obtain_pair'),
    path('api/token/refresh/', TokenRefreshView.as_view(), name='token_refresh'),
]
```

Now, React can request a **JWT token** by sending a POST request to /api/token/.

Step 3: Handle Login in React

Modify src/Login.js:

javascript
CopyEdit
```javascript
import React, { useState } from "react";
import axios from "axios";

const Login = () => {
  const [credentials, setCredentials] = useState({ username: "", password: "" });
  const [token, setToken] = useState("");
```

```
const handleChange = (e) => {
  setCredentials({ ...credentials, [e.target.name]: e.target.value });
};

const handleSubmit = (e) => {
  e.preventDefault();
  axios.post("http://127.0.0.1:8000/api/token/", credentials)
    .then(response => setToken(response.data.access))
    .catch(error => console.error("Login failed:", error));
};

return (
  <div>
    <h2>Login</h2>
    <form onSubmit={handleSubmit}>
      <input type="text" name="username" placeholder="Username"
onChange={handleChange} />
      <input type="password" name="password" placeholder="Password"
onChange={handleChange} />
      <button type="submit">Login</button>
    </form>
    {token && <p>Token: {token}</p>}
  </div>
);
};

export default Login;
```

■ Sends credentials to /api/token/ to obtain a JWT token.
■ Stores the token in React **state** for authentication.

2.4 Using JWT Token to Access Protected APIs

Modify src/App.js to send the token in API requests:

```javascript
CopyEdit
axios.get("http://127.0.0.1:8000/api/posts/", {
  headers: { Authorization: `Bearer ${token}` }
});
```

Now, users **must be logged in** to fetch blog posts.

Handling CORS Issues in Django

By default, Django's security settings **block cross-origin requests**. This means that a **React or Vue.js frontend (running on** localhost:3000) cannot access a Django API on localhost:8000 unless explicitly allowed.

1.1 What is CORS?

CORS (Cross-Origin Resource Sharing) is a security mechanism that prevents **unauthorized domains** from making API requests to your Django backend.

Example **CORS error** in the browser console:

```sh
CopyEdit
Access to fetch at 'http://127.0.0.1:8000/api/posts/' from origin 'http://localhost:3000' has
been blocked by CORS policy.
```

■ To fix this, Django must **explicitly allow** requests from the frontend domain.

1.2 Installing and Configuring django-cors-headers

Step 1: Install django-cors-headers

sh

CopyEdit

```
pip install django-cors-headers
```

Step 2: Add corsheaders to Installed Apps

Modify settings.py:

python

CopyEdit

```
INSTALLED_APPS += ['corsheaders']
```

Step 3: Add CORS Middleware

Modify MIDDLEWARE:

python

CopyEdit

```
MIDDLEWARE += ['corsheaders.middleware.CorsMiddleware']
```

219

Step 4: Allow Specific Frontend Domains

Modify settings.py:

python

CopyEdit

```
CORS_ALLOWED_ORIGINS = [

    "http://localhost:3000",  # React frontend

    "http://localhost:5173",  # Vue.js frontend

]
```

■ Now, requests from **React (localhost:3000) and Vue.js (localhost:5173)** will be allowed.

1.3 Allowing All Origins (For Development Only!)

To allow **any domain** (useful for local testing):

python

CopyEdit

```
CORS_ALLOW_ALL_ORIGINS = True  # WARNING: Only use in development!
```

▲ **Do not enable this in production** to prevent **security risks**.

1.4 Allowing Specific HTTP Methods and Headers

To restrict CORS to **specific HTTP methods**, modify settings.py:

python

CopyEdit

```
CORS_ALLOW_METHODS = [

    "GET",

    "POST",

    "PUT",

    "DELETE",

]


CORS_ALLOW_HEADERS = [

    "content-type",

    "authorization",

]
```

■ This ensures **only selected methods** are allowed from the frontend.

1.5 Testing CORS Configuration

Restart Django:

sh

CopyEdit

```
python manage.py runserver
```

Then, test from **React or Vue.js**:

javascript

CopyEdit

```
fetch("http://127.0.0.1:8000/api/posts/")
  .then(response => response.json())
  .then(data => console.log(data))
  .catch(error => console.error("CORS error:", error));
```

If everything is configured correctly, Django should **return JSON data** without CORS errors.

Using Django with Vue.js and HTMX for Server-Side Rendering

Django integrates well with **both Vue.js and HTMX,** allowing developers to choose between **SPA (Single Page Applications) and SSR (Server-Side Rendering).**

2.1 Setting Up Django with Vue.js

Vue.js provides a **lightweight frontend framework** that can work as:
■ A **standalone SPA** (fetching data via Django REST API).
■ A **server-rendered frontend** (embedded into Django templates).

2.2 Setting Up Vue.js for Django Backend

Step 1: Create a Vue.js Project

sh

CopyEdit

```
npm create vue@latest myfrontend

cd myfrontend

npm install

npm run dev
```

Vue.js will start at http://localhost:5173.

Step 2: Fetch Data from Django API in Vue.js

Modify src/App.vue:

vue

CopyEdit

```
<script setup>

import { ref, onMounted } from "vue";
```

```
const posts = ref([]);

onMounted(() => {
  fetch("http://127.0.0.1:8000/api/posts/")
    .then(response => response.json())
    .then(data => (posts.value = data));
});
</script>

<template>
  <h1>Blog Posts</h1>
  <ul>
    <li v-for="post in posts" :key="post.id">{{ post.title }}</li>
  </ul>
</template>
```

■ Vue.js will **fetch data from Django's API** and display it in the UI.

2.3 Using Vue.js Inside Django Templates (SSR Approach)

Instead of running Vue.js separately, embed it inside Django's templates.

Modify base.html:

html

CopyEdit

```html
<!DOCTYPE html>
<html>
<head>
  <title>Vue + Django</title>
  <script src="https://cdn.jsdelivr.net/npm/vue@3/dist/vue.global.js"></script>
</head>
<body>
  <div id="app">
    <h1>{{ message }}</h1>
  </div>

  <script>
    Vue.createApp({
      data() {
        return { message: "Hello from Vue inside Django!" };
      }
    }).mount("#app");
```

```
    </script>

</body>

</html>
```

■ Vue **renders inside Django templates**, keeping Django's server-side rendering intact.

3. Using Django with HTMX for Server-Side Rendering

HTMX allows **dynamic page updates** without requiring a full **JavaScript frontend framework**.

■ No need for **React or Vue.js**.
■ **Minimal JavaScript** required.
■ **Server-Side Rendering (SSR)** with Django templates.

3.1 Installing HTMX

Include HTMX in your Django template:

html

CopyEdit

```
<script src="https://unpkg.com/htmx.org@1.9.4"></script>
```

■ No extra installation needed!

3.2 Using HTMX for Dynamic Content Updates

Instead of **fetching data via JavaScript**, HTMX allows Django to **return partial HTML responses**.

Example: Load Blog Posts Dynamically with HTMX

Modify views.py:

python

CopyEdit

```python
from django.shortcuts import render
from .models import BlogPost


def blog_list(request):
    posts = BlogPost.objects.all()
    return render(request, "blog_list.html", {"posts": posts})
```

Modify urls.py:

python

CopyEdit

```python
from django.urls import path
from .views import blog_list


urlpatterns = [
    path("blog/", blog_list, name="blog_list"),
]
```

227

Modify blog_list.html:

html

CopyEdit

```
<ul id="blog-posts">
    {% for post in posts %}
        <li>{{ post.title }}</li>
    {% endfor %}
</ul>


<button hx-get="/blog/" hx-target="#blog-posts" hx-swap="outerHTML">
    Refresh Posts
</button>
```

■ Clicking the button **updates the blog post list dynamically** without reloading the page.

Chapter 11: Deploying Django Applications

Deploying a Django application involves **optimizing performance, securing configurations, and choosing the right hosting service**. Whether deploying on **AWS (EC2, Elastic Beanstalk), DigitalOcean, Heroku, or a VPS**, proper preparation ensures a smooth transition from development to production.

Preparing a Django App for Production

Before deploying, we must ensure Django is **secure, optimized, and properly configured**.

1.1 Switching to Production Settings

Modify settings.py:

Enable Debug Mode for Development, Disable for Production
python
CopyEdit
DEBUG = False # Set to False in production

Use a Strong Secret Key in Production
python
CopyEdit
import os
SECRET_KEY = os.getenv("DJANGO_SECRET_KEY", "your-secret-key")

Store **environment variables** using .env files or AWS Secrets Manager.

1.2 Allowing Specific Hosts

Restrict access to trusted domains:

python
CopyEdit
ALLOWED_HOSTS = ["yourdomain.com", "your-api.com"]

229

To allow **all hosts** (only for debugging):

```python
CopyEdit
ALLOWED_HOSTS = ["*"]  # WARNING: Do not use in production
```

1.3 Configuring Static and Media Files

Serve Static Files in Production

Use **WhiteNoise** for efficient static file serving:

```sh
CopyEdit
pip install whitenoise
```

Modify MIDDLEWARE:

```python
CopyEdit
MIDDLEWARE.insert(1, "whitenoise.middleware.WhiteNoiseMiddleware")
```

Run:

```sh
CopyEdit
python manage.py collectstatic
```

Now, static files are served **efficiently in production**.

1.4 Using a Production Database

SQLite is not recommended for production. Use **PostgreSQL or MySQL**.

Install PostgreSQL

sh
CopyEdit
```
pip install psycopg2-binary
```

Modify Database Configuration (settings.py)

python
CopyEdit
```
DATABASES = {
    "default": {
        "ENGINE": "django.db.backends.postgresql",
        "NAME": "dbname",
        "USER": "dbuser",
        "PASSWORD": "dbpassword",
        "HOST": "your-database-host",
        "PORT": "5432",
    }
}
```

Run migrations:

sh
CopyEdit
```
python manage.py migrate
```

1.5 Setting Up Gunicorn for WSGI Application

Gunicorn is a **high-performance Python WSGI server**.

Install Gunicorn:

sh
CopyEdit
```
pip install gunicorn
```

Run Gunicorn:

sh
CopyEdit
```
gunicorn myproject.wsgi:application --bind 0.0.0.0:8000
```

1.6 Enforcing Security Measures

Use HTTPS with Secure Cookies
python
CopyEdit
```python
CSRF_COOKIE_SECURE = True
SESSION_COOKIE_SECURE = True
SECURE_SSL_REDIRECT = True
```

Enable Content Security Policy (CSP)
python
CopyEdit
```python
CSP_DEFAULT_SRC = ("'self'",)
CSP_SCRIPT_SRC = ("'self'", "'unsafe-inline'")
```

Install CSP middleware:

sh
CopyEdit
```
pip install django-csp
```

1.7 Using a Reverse Proxy with Nginx

Nginx handles **static files, SSL, and request forwarding**.

Create an Nginx configuration file (/etc/nginx/sites-available/myproject):

nginx
CopyEdit
```nginx
server {
```

```
listen 80;
server_name yourdomain.com;

location / {
    proxy_pass http://127.0.0.1:8000;
    proxy_set_header Host $host;
    proxy_set_header X-Real-IP $remote_addr;
    proxy_set_header X-Forwarded-For $proxy_add_x_forwarded_for;
}

location /static/ {
    alias /home/ubuntu/myproject/staticfiles/;
}
}
```

Restart Nginx:

sh
CopyEdit
```
sudo systemctl restart nginx
```

Deploying on AWS (EC2, Elastic Beanstalk)

AWS offers **scalable deployment options**, including **EC2 (manual setup)** and **Elastic Beanstalk (fully managed deployment).**

2.1 Deploying Django on AWS EC2

Step 1: Create an EC2 Instance

1. Log in to AWS and navigate to **EC2**.
2. Click **Launch Instance**.
3. Choose **Ubuntu 22.04** as the OS.
4. Select **t2.micro** (Free Tier eligible).
5. Configure **security group rules**:
   - Allow **HTTP (80)** and **HTTPS (443)**.
   - Allow **SSH (22)** only for your IP.

233

Step 2: Connect to the EC2 Instance

After launching, connect via SSH:

```sh
CopyEdit
ssh -i mykey.pem ubuntu@your-ec2-public-ip
```

Step 3: Install Required Packages

Update packages:

```sh
CopyEdit
sudo apt update && sudo apt upgrade -y
```

Install dependencies:

```sh
CopyEdit
sudo apt install python3-pip python3-venv nginx postgresql -y
```

Create a **Python virtual environment**:

```sh
CopyEdit
python3 -m venv myenv
source myenv/bin/activate
```

Step 4: Clone Django Project and Install Dependencies

Clone from **GitHub**:

```sh
CopyEdit
git clone https://github.com/yourusername/myproject.git
cd myproject
```

234

Install dependencies:

sh
CopyEdit
pip install -r requirements.txt

Run migrations:

sh
CopyEdit
python manage.py migrate

Collect static files:

sh
CopyEdit
python manage.py collectstatic

Step 5: Set Up Gunicorn and Nginx

Run Gunicorn:

sh
CopyEdit
gunicorn myproject.wsgi:application --bind 0.0.0.0:8000

Configure **Nginx** (as shown earlier).

Step 6: Start Django as a System Service

Create a **Gunicorn service file** (/etc/systemd/system/gunicorn.service):

ini
CopyEdit
[Unit]
Description=Gunicorn service for Django
After=network.target

235

```
[Service]
User=ubuntu
Group=ubuntu
WorkingDirectory=/home/ubuntu/myproject
ExecStart=/home/ubuntu/myenv/bin/gunicorn --workers 3 --bind
unix:/home/ubuntu/myproject.sock myproject.wsgi:application

[Install]
WantedBy=multi-user.target
```

Start and enable the service:

sh
CopyEdit
```
sudo systemctl start gunicorn
sudo systemctl enable gunicorn
```

Restart Nginx:

sh
CopyEdit
```
sudo systemctl restart nginx
```

■ Django is now deployed on **AWS EC2**.

2.2 Deploying Django on AWS Elastic Beanstalk

AWS Elastic Beanstalk automates deployment.

Step 1: Install AWS CLI and EB CLI
sh
CopyEdit
```
pip install awsebcli --upgrade
```

Step 2: Initialize Elastic Beanstalk

Inside your Django project, run:

sh
CopyEdit
eb init -p python-3.8 my-django-app

Choose **AWS region and application name**.

Step 3: Deploy the App

Run:

sh
CopyEdit
eb create my-env

Elastic Beanstalk will:
■ Provision EC2, RDS, and Load Balancers.
■ Deploy Django automatically.

To update the app later:

sh
CopyEdit
eb deploy

■ Your Django app is **live on AWS Beanstalk**.

Deploying on Heroku, DigitalOcean, and VPS Servers

1.1 Deploying Django on Heroku

Heroku is a **Platform-as-a-Service (PaaS)** that simplifies Django deployment without requiring server management.

Step 1: Install Heroku CLI and Dependencies

Install the Heroku CLI:

sh
CopyEdit
curl https://cli-assets.heroku.com/install.sh | sh

Log in:

sh
CopyEdit
heroku login

Install **Gunicorn** and **dj-database-url** for database configuration:

sh
CopyEdit
pip install gunicorn dj-database-url

Step 2: Prepare requirements.txt

Generate or update the requirements.txt file:

sh
CopyEdit
pip freeze > requirements.txt

Step 3: Configure Procfile

Create a Procfile in the root directory of your project:

ini
CopyEdit
web: gunicorn myproject.wsgi --log-file -

Step 4: Configure the Database for Heroku

Modify settings.py:

python
CopyEdit
```python
import dj_database_url
DATABASES['default'] = dj_database_url.config(conn_max_age=600, ssl_require=True)
```

Step 5: Initialize Git and Push to Heroku

Initialize a Git repository:

sh
CopyEdit
```sh
git init
git add .
git commit -m "Deploy Django to Heroku"
```

Create a Heroku app:

sh
CopyEdit
```sh
heroku create my-django-app
```

Push the project to Heroku:

sh
CopyEdit
```sh
git push heroku main
```

Step 6: Run Migrations and Scale the App
sh
CopyEdit
```sh
heroku run python manage.py migrate
```

239

```
heroku ps:scale web=1
heroku open
```

■ Your Django app is now live on Heroku!

1.2 Deploying Django on DigitalOcean

DigitalOcean provides **affordable VPS instances (Droplets)** with more control than Heroku.

Step 1: Create a DigitalOcean Droplet

1. Log in to DigitalOcean.
2. Create a new **Ubuntu 22.04 Droplet**.
3. Set up an SSH key and launch the server.
4. Connect to the server:

sh
CopyEdit
```
ssh root@your-server-ip
```


Step 2: Install Dependencies

Update system packages:

sh
CopyEdit
```
sudo apt update && sudo apt upgrade -y
```


Install Python, Nginx, PostgreSQL, and required dependencies:

sh
CopyEdit
```
sudo apt install python3-pip python3-venv nginx postgresql -y
```

Step 3: Set Up a Virtual Environment

sh
CopyEdit

```
python3 -m venv venv
source venv/bin/activate
pip install -r requirements.txt
```

Step 4: Set Up Gunicorn

sh
CopyEdit

```
pip install gunicorn
gunicorn --bind 0.0.0.0:8000 myproject.wsgi
```

Step 5: Set Up PostgreSQL Database

Login to PostgreSQL:

sh
CopyEdit

```
sudo -u postgres psql
```

Create a new database and user:

sql
CopyEdit

```
CREATE DATABASE mydatabase;
CREATE USER myuser WITH ENCRYPTED PASSWORD 'mypassword';
GRANT ALL PRIVILEGES ON DATABASE mydatabase TO myuser;
```

Modify settings.py:

python
CopyEdit

```
DATABASES = {
    "default": {
        "ENGINE": "django.db.backends.postgresql",
        "NAME": "mydatabase",
```

241

```
    "USER": "myuser",
    "PASSWORD": "mypassword",
    "HOST": "localhost",
    "PORT": "5432",
  }
}
```

Apply migrations:

sh
CopyEdit
```
python manage.py migrate
```

Step 6: Configure Gunicorn as a System Service

Create a Gunicorn service file:

sh
CopyEdit
```
sudo nano /etc/systemd/system/gunicorn.service
```

Add the following:

ini
CopyEdit
```
[Unit]
Description=Gunicorn for Django
After=network.target

[Service]
User=root
WorkingDirectory=/root/myproject
ExecStart=/root/venv/bin/gunicorn --workers 3 --bind unix:/root/myproject.sock myproject.wsgi:application

[Install]
WantedBy=multi-user.target
```

242

Enable and start the service:

sh
CopyEdit
sudo systemctl start gunicorn
sudo systemctl enable gunicorn

■ Django is now running on **DigitalOcean VPS**.

1.3 Deploying Django on a VPS Server

A VPS allows **full control** over the deployment process.

1. **Choose a VPS provider** – AWS Lightsail, Linode, or Vultr.
2. **Follow DigitalOcean deployment steps** – Setup Ubuntu, install Gunicorn, PostgreSQL, and Nginx.
3. **Configure DNS and SSL using Let's Encrypt**:

sh
CopyEdit
sudo apt install certbot python3-certbot-nginx
sudo certbot --nginx -d yourdomain.com

■ Your Django app is now running **securely on a VPS**.

Setting Up a Production Environment with Nginx and Gunicorn

Gunicorn handles **Django application requests**, while **Nginx serves static files and proxies requests**.

2.1 Installing and Configuring Nginx

Install Nginx:

sh
CopyEdit
sudo apt install nginx -y

243

Create an Nginx configuration file:

sh
CopyEdit
sudo nano /etc/nginx/sites-available/myproject

Add the following configuration:

nginx
CopyEdit
```
server {
    listen 80;
    server_name yourdomain.com;

    location / {
        proxy_pass http://127.0.0.1:8000;
        proxy_set_header Host $host;
        proxy_set_header X-Real-IP $remote_addr;
        proxy_set_header X-Forwarded-For $proxy_add_x_forwarded_for;
    }

    location /static/ {
        alias /root/myproject/staticfiles/;
    }
}
```

Enable the configuration:

sh
CopyEdit
```
sudo ln -s /etc/nginx/sites-available/myproject /etc/nginx/sites-enabled/
sudo nginx -t
sudo systemctl restart nginx
```

2.2 Running Django with Gunicorn

Run Gunicorn:

sh
CopyEdit
```
gunicorn --workers 3 --bind unix:/root/myproject.sock myproject.wsgi:application
```

Ensure Gunicorn runs on **server startup**:

sh
CopyEdit
```
sudo systemctl enable gunicorn
```

2.3 Using Supervisor to Manage Gunicorn

Install Supervisor:

sh
CopyEdit
```
sudo apt install supervisor -y
```

Create a Supervisor configuration file:

sh
CopyEdit
```
sudo nano /etc/supervisor/conf.d/myproject.conf
```

Add:

ini
CopyEdit
```
[program:myproject]
command=/root/venv/bin/gunicorn --workers 3 --bind unix:/root/myproject.sock
myproject.wsgi:application
directory=/root/myproject
autostart=true
```

245

```
autorestart=true
stderr_logfile=/var/log/myproject.err.log
stdout_logfile=/var/log/myproject.out.log
```

Reload Supervisor:

sh

CopyEdit

```
sudo supervisorctl reread
sudo supervisorctl update
sudo supervisorctl start myproject
```

█ Django will now restart **automatically on crashes**.

CI/CD Pipelines for Django Projects (GitHub Actions, GitLab CI)

CI/CD pipelines **automate**: █ **Testing Django code** before deployment.
█ **Building and packaging** Django applications.
█ **Deploying Django to AWS, Heroku, or a VPS**.

1.1 Setting Up CI/CD with GitHub Actions

GitHub Actions automates testing and deployment.

Step 1: Create a .github/workflows/django.yml **File**

Inside your Django project, create:

sh

CopyEdit

```
mkdir -p .github/workflows

nano .github/workflows/django.yml
```

246

Step 2: Define the Workflow for Testing and Deployment

yaml

CopyEdit

name: Django CI/CD

on:
  push:
    branches:
      - main
  pull_request:
    branches:
      - main

jobs:
  test:
    runs-on: ubuntu-latest
    steps:
      - name: Checkout code
        uses: actions/checkout@v3

      - name: Set up Python
        uses: actions/setup-python@v3

247

```yaml
    with:
      python-version: '3.9'

  - name: Install dependencies
    run: |
      pip install --upgrade pip
      pip install -r requirements.txt

  - name: Run Django tests
    run: |
      python manage.py test

deploy:
  needs: test
  runs-on: ubuntu-latest
  if: github.ref == 'refs/heads/main'
  steps:
    - name: Deploy to Production
      run: |
        ssh ubuntu@your-server-ip 'cd /home/ubuntu/myproject && git pull origin main && sudo systemctl restart gunicorn'
```

■ This pipeline.

- Runs Django tests on **every push**.
- Deploys to a **VPS server (Ubuntu)** if tests pass.

1.2 Setting Up CI/CD with GitLab CI

GitLab has built-in **CI/CD pipelines**.

Step 1: Create .gitlab-ci.yml in Your Repository

sh

CopyEdit

```
nano .gitlab-ci.yml
```

Step 2: Define the GitLab CI/CD Pipeline

yaml

CopyEdit

```
stages:
  - test
  - deploy


test:
  image: python:3.9
  before_script:
    - pip install --upgrade pip
    - pip install -r requirements.txt
  script:
```

249

```
- python manage.py test


deploy:

  stage: deploy

  only:

    - main

  script:

    - ssh ubuntu@your-server-ip 'cd /home/ubuntu/myproject && git pull origin main
&& sudo systemctl restart gunicorn'
```

■ **GitLab CI/CD** runs tests and deploys automatically.

1.3 Deploying Django to Heroku with GitHub Actions

To **deploy automatically** to Heroku:

1. Add **Heroku API Key** as a **GitHub Secret**.
2. Modify .github/workflows/django.yml:

yaml

CopyEdit

```
deploy:

  needs: test

  runs-on: ubuntu-latest

  steps:

    - name: Deploy to Heroku
```

```
env:

  HEROKU_API_KEY: ${{ secrets.HEROKU_API_KEY }}

run: |

  heroku container:login

  heroku container:push web --app your-heroku-app

  heroku container:release web --app your-heroku-app
```

■ Now, Django **deploys to Heroku automatically** when pushed to main.

Using Docker and Kubernetes with Django

2.1 Why Use Docker for Django?

■ **Ensures consistency** across development, testing, and production.
■ **Removes dependency conflicts** with isolated containers.
■ **Easily deployable** to **AWS, Kubernetes, and Docker Swarm**.

2.2 Writing a Dockerfile for Django

Inside the Django project, create a Dockerfile:

sh

CopyEdit

```
nano Dockerfile
```

Step 1: Define the Dockerfile

dockerfile

CopyEdit

```
# Use an official Python runtime
```

251

```
FROM python:3.9

# Set environment variables
ENV PYTHONUNBUFFERED 1

# Set the working directory
WORKDIR /app

# Copy project files
COPY . /app/

# Install dependencies
RUN pip install --upgrade pip
RUN pip install -r requirements.txt

# Run Django server
CMD ["gunicorn", "--bind", "0.0.0.0:8000", "myproject.wsgi"]
```

■ **This builds a Docker image** for Django.

2.3 Creating a docker-compose.yml File

Docker Compose simplifies **running Django, PostgreSQL, and Redis** in containers.

sh

CopyEdit

nano docker-compose.yml

Step 1: Define Services in docker-compose.yml

yaml

CopyEdit

```
version: '3.8'

services:
  web:
    build: .
    container_name: django_app
    command: gunicorn --bind 0.0.0.0:8000 myproject.wsgi
    ports:
      - "8000:8000"
    depends_on:
      - db
    env_file:
      - .env

  db:
```

253

```
image: postgres:13

container_name: django_db

environment:

  POSTGRES_USER: myuser

  POSTGRES_PASSWORD: mypassword

  POSTGRES_DB: mydatabase

ports:

  - "5432:5432"
```

■ **This creates two containers**:

1. web – Runs Django with Gunicorn.
2. db – Uses PostgreSQL as a database.

2.4 Running Django with Docker

Step 1: Build the Docker Image

sh

CopyEdit

```
docker-compose build
```

Step 2: Run the Containers

sh

CopyEdit

```
docker-compose up -d
```

■ Django now runs in **Docker containers**.

3. Deploying Django on Kubernetes

Kubernetes manages **multiple Django containers** efficiently.

3.1 Writing a Kubernetes Deployment File

Create django-deployment.yml:

yaml

CopyEdit

```yaml
apiVersion: apps/v1
kind: Deployment
metadata:
  name: django-app
spec:
  replicas: 3
  selector:
    matchLabels:
      app: django
  template:
    metadata:
      labels:
        app: django
    spec:
```

```
containers:

- name: django

  image: my-django-image

  ports:

  - containerPort: 8000
```

3.2 Deploying Django to Kubernetes

Step 1: Apply the Deployment

sh

CopyEdit

```
kubectl apply -f django-deployment.yml
```

Step 2: Expose Django as a Service

sh

CopyEdit

```
kubectl expose deployment django-app --type=LoadBalancer --port=8000
```

■ Now, Django runs in a **Kubernetes cluster**.

Chapter 12: Security Best Practices in Django

Web security is a **critical aspect** of Django development. Django includes **built-in security mechanisms** to protect applications from **SQL injection, XSS (Cross-Site Scripting), CSRF (Cross-Site Request Forgery), Clickjacking, and other vulnerabilities**.

Protecting Against SQL Injection, XSS, CSRF, and Clickjacking

Modern web applications **face constant threats** from malicious attacks. Django provides built-in tools to **mitigate these risks**.

1.1 Preventing SQL Injection

SQL Injection occurs when **malicious SQL queries** manipulate a database by injecting harmful inputs.

Example of SQL Injection Vulnerability

python
CopyEdit

```python
def search_user(request):
    username = request.GET.get('username')
    query = f"SELECT * FROM users WHERE username = '{username}'"
    cursor.execute(query)  # UNSAFE!
```

If a user enters:

sh
CopyEdit

```sh
' OR 1=1 --
```

The database executes:

sql
CopyEdit

```sql
SELECT * FROM users WHERE username = '' OR 1=1 --'
```

This allows **attackers to bypass authentication**.

■ Solution: Use Django's ORM Instead of Raw Queries

python
CopyEdit

```python
from django.shortcuts import get_object_or_404
from .models import User

def search_user(request):
    username = request.GET.get('username')
    user = get_object_or_404(User, username=username)
    return JsonResponse({'id': user.id, 'name': user.username})
```

■ Avoid raw() Queries Unless Necessary

python
CopyEdit

```python
User.objects.raw("SELECT * FROM users WHERE username = %s", [username])
```

1.2 Preventing XSS (Cross-Site Scripting) Attacks

XSS (Cross-Site Scripting) allows attackers to **inject malicious JavaScript** into web pages, executing scripts in users' browsers.

Example of XSS Vulnerability
html
CopyEdit

```html
<form>
    <input type="text" name="message">
    <p>Your Message: {{ request.GET.message }}</p>  <!-- UNSAFE -->
</form>
```

If a user enters:

html
CopyEdit
```
<script>alert("Hacked!")</script>
```

The browser executes the JavaScript **inside the application**.

■ Solution: Django Auto-Escapes Output in Templates

Django **escapes all user input** by default:

html
CopyEdit
```
<p>Your Message: {{ request.GET.message }}</p>  <!-- SAFE -->
```

■ Use mark_safe Cautiously

python
CopyEdit
```
from django.utils.safestring import mark_safe

message = "<strong>Hello</strong>"
safe_message = mark_safe(message)  # Be careful when using this!
```

■ Sanitize Input Using bleach Library

sh
CopyEdit
```
pip install bleach
```

python
CopyEdit
```
import bleach

user_input = request.GET.get('message')
```

259

```
safe_input = bleach.clean(user_input)  # Removes harmful scripts
```

1.3 Preventing CSRF (Cross-Site Request Forgery) Attacks

CSRF (Cross-Site Request Forgery) tricks users into performing unwanted actions **without their consent**.

Example of CSRF Attack

1. User logs into **bank.com**.
2. A malicious website sends a **POST request** in the background:

html
CopyEdit
```html
<form action="https://bank.com/transfer/" method="POST">
   <input type="hidden" name="amount" value="1000">
   <input type="hidden" name="recipient" value="attacker">
</form>
```

3. The bank executes the request **because the user is authenticated**.

■ Solution: Enable CSRF Protection in Django

Django **includes CSRF protection** by default.

Use the {% csrf_token %} tag in forms:

html
CopyEdit
```html
<form method="POST">
   {% csrf_token %}
   <input type="text" name="message">
   <button type="submit">Submit</button>
</form>
```

◼ CSRF Protection for API Endpoints

For Django REST Framework APIs, use **CSRF exempt when needed**:

python
CopyEdit
```python
from django.views.decorators.csrf import csrf_exempt

@csrf_exempt
def my_view(request):
    return JsonResponse({'message': 'CSRF disabled'})
```

◼ Use CSRF Protection in JavaScript Requests

javascript
CopyEdit
```javascript
fetch('/api/data/', {
    method: "POST",
    headers: {
        "X-CSRFToken": getCookie("csrftoken")
    },
    body: JSON.stringify(data)
});
```

1.4 Preventing Clickjacking Attacks

Clickjacking tricks users into **clicking hidden buttons** within **an invisible iframe**, hijacking their actions.

Example of Clickjacking

An attacker embeds your site inside their malicious site:

html
CopyEdit
```html
<iframe src="https://secure-site.com" width="100%" height="100%" style="opacity:0.1;"></iframe>
```

Users unknowingly **interact with your site through the attacker's page**.

261

■ **Solution: Use the X-Frame-Options Header**

Django provides X-Frame-Options by default.

Modify settings.py:

```python
CopyEdit
X_FRAME_OPTIONS = 'DENY'
```

■ **Or Allow Clickjacking Only from Trusted Sources**

```python
CopyEdit
X_FRAME_OPTIONS = 'SAMEORIGIN' # Allows embedding from the same domain
```

Using Django's Security Middleware

Django provides **Security Middleware** to enforce **best security practices**.

2.1 Enabling Django Security Middleware

Modify MIDDLEWARE in settings.py:

```python
CopyEdit
MIDDLEWARE = [
    "django.middleware.security.SecurityMiddleware",
    "django.middleware.csrf.CsrfViewMiddleware",
    "django.middleware.clickjacking.XFrameOptionsMiddleware",
]
```

■ **SecurityMiddleware** – Protects against common security threats.
■ **CsrfViewMiddleware** – Enables **CSRF protection**.
■ **XFrameOptionsMiddleware** – Prevents **clickjacking attacks**.

2.2 Enforcing HTTPS (SSL/TLS Encryption)

Django should **force HTTPS connections**.

Modify settings.py:

python
CopyEdit
```
SECURE_SSL_REDIRECT = True  # Redirect HTTP to HTTPS
SECURE_HSTS_SECONDS = 31536000  # Enforce HTTPS for 1 year
SECURE_HSTS_INCLUDE_SUBDOMAINS = True
SECURE_HSTS_PRELOAD = True
```

■ This **forces all traffic over HTTPS**, protecting **user data**.

2.3 Setting Secure Cookies

Cookies should **only be sent over secure HTTPS connections**.

Modify settings.py:

python
CopyEdit
```
SESSION_COOKIE_SECURE = True
CSRF_COOKIE_SECURE = True
```

■ **Prevents session hijacking** over **unencrypted connections**.

2.4 Using Content Security Policy (CSP) to Prevent XSS

The **Content Security Policy (CSP)** restricts **JavaScript execution**.

Install Django CSP:

sh
CopyEdit
```
pip install django-csp
```

263

Modify settings.py:

python
CopyEdit
CSP_DEFAULT_SRC = ("'self'",) # Allow scripts from the same domain
CSP_SCRIPT_SRC = ("'self'", "'unsafe-inline'") # Restrict external scripts
CSP_STYLE_SRC = ("'self'", "https://fonts.googleapis.com") # Allow Google Fonts

■ **Blocks malicious JavaScript injections**.

Secure Handling of Sensitive Data

1.1 Storing Credentials Securely

Django applications **should never store sensitive information in the codebase**.

✖ **Bad Practice (Hardcoded Credentials in settings.py)**

python

CopyEdit

```
DATABASES = {

    "default": {

        "ENGINE": "django.db.backends.postgresql",

        "NAME": "mydatabase",

        "USER": "myuser",

        "PASSWORD": "mypassword",

    }

}
```

Storing credentials in code **exposes** them if the repository is leaked.

1.2 Using Environment Variables for Security

Use **.env files** to store credentials securely.

Step 1: Install python-dotenv

sh

CopyEdit

```
pip install python-dotenv
```

Step 2: Create a .env File

ini

CopyEdit

```
DATABASE_NAME=mydatabase

DATABASE_USER=myuser

DATABASE_PASSWORD=mypassword

SECRET_KEY=my-secret-key
```

Step 3: Load .env in settings.py

python

CopyEdit

```
import os

from dotenv import load_dotenv
```

265

```python
load_dotenv()

DATABASES = {
    "default": {
        "ENGINE": "django.db.backends.postgresql",
        "NAME": os.getenv("DATABASE_NAME"),
        "USER": os.getenv("DATABASE_USER"),
        "PASSWORD": os.getenv("DATABASE_PASSWORD"),
    }
}


SECRET_KEY = os.getenv("SECRET_KEY")
```

■ **Benefits**:

- **No sensitive data in code.**
- **Easier environment management (Development vs. Production).**

1.3 Encrypting Sensitive Data

Never store raw sensitive information in the database.

Use Django's Cryptographic Module for Encryption

python

CopyEdit

```python
from django.core.signing import Signer
```

```
signer = Signer()
encrypted_data = signer.sign("Sensitive Information")
print(encrypted_data)
```

Decryption:

python

CopyEdit

```
print(signer.unsign(encrypted_data))
```

■ **Protects** against **database leaks**.

1.4 Using Django's Secure Password Storage

Django uses **PBKDF2** for hashing passwords.

■ **Always use Django's built-in authentication**:

python

CopyEdit

```
from django.contrib.auth.models import User

user = User.objects.create_user(username="john", password="securepassword")
```

■ **Never store plaintext passwords**.

Implementing Rate Limiting and Secure API Endpoints

Rate limiting protects APIs from: ■ **DDoS attacks**
■ **Brute-force attempts**
■ **Excessive traffic**

2.1 Setting Up Rate Limiting with django-ratelimit

Install:

sh

CopyEdit

```
pip install django-ratelimit
```

Example: Limit Login Attempts

Modify views.py:

python

CopyEdit

```
from django_ratelimit.decorators import ratelimit
from django.http import JsonResponse


@ratelimit(key="ip", rate="5/m", method="POST", block=True)
def login_view(request):
    return JsonResponse({"message": "Login successful"})
```

■ **Limits to 5 login attempts per minute per IP**.

2.2 Secure API Endpoints with Django REST Framework

Django REST Framework (DRF) provides: ■ **Authentication (Token, JWT, OAuth)**
■ **Permissions (IsAuthenticated, IsAdminUser)**
■ **Rate Limiting**

2.2.1 Enforcing Authentication

Modify settings.py:

python

CopyEdit

```python
REST_FRAMEWORK = {

  "DEFAULT_AUTHENTICATION_CLASSES": [

    "rest_framework.authentication.TokenAuthentication",

  ],

  "DEFAULT_PERMISSION_CLASSES": [

    "rest_framework.permissions.IsAuthenticated",

  ],

}
```

■ **Only authenticated users can access the API.**

2.2.2 Using JWT for Secure API Authentication

Install:

sh

CopyEdit

```sh
pip install djangorestframework-simplejwt
```

269

Modify settings.py:

python

CopyEdit

```
from datetime import timedelta


REST_FRAMEWORK["DEFAULT_AUTHENTICATION_CLASSES"].append(
    "rest_framework_simplejwt.authentication.JWTAuthentication"
)


SIMPLE_JWT = {
    "ACCESS_TOKEN_LIFETIME": timedelta(days=1),
}
```

■ Users authenticate via **JWT tokens**.

2.2.3 Enforcing Role-Based Access Control (RBAC)

Modify permissions.py:

python

CopyEdit

```
from rest_framework.permissions import BasePermission


class IsAdminOrReadOnly(BasePermission):
    def has_permission(self, request, view):
```

```python
return request.method in ["GET"] or request.user.is_staff
```

Apply to views:

python

CopyEdit

```python
from rest_framework.decorators import api_view, permission_classes


@api_view(["GET", "POST"])
@permission_classes([IsAdminOrReadOnly])
def my_api_view(request):
    return JsonResponse({"message": "Secure API"})
```

■ **Only admins can create data**, others can only read.

2.3 Preventing API Data Leaks

Restrict **sensitive fields** in serializers:

python

CopyEdit

```python
from rest_framework import serializers
from .models import User


class UserSerializer(serializers.ModelSerializer):
    class Meta:
```

271

```python
model = User

exclude = ["password", "email"]
```

■ Prevents **leaking sensitive information**.

2.4 Hiding API Endpoints from Hackers

Remove Browsable API to prevent attackers from exploring your API.

Modify settings.py:

python

CopyEdit

```python
REST_FRAMEWORK["DEFAULT_RENDERER_CLASSES"] = [

    "rest_framework.renderers.JSONRenderer",

]
```

■ **API returns only JSON**, hiding unnecessary UI.

Chapter 13: Advanced Django Topics

Django provides powerful features for building **scalable and flexible applications**. Two advanced concepts that are widely used in **modern web development** include:

1. **Multi-Tenant Architecture in Django (Building SaaS Applications)** – Creating applications that serve multiple customers from a single codebase.
2. **Django and GraphQL Integration** – Using GraphQL for more efficient and flexible data retrieval.

Multi-Tenant Architecture in Django (Building SaaS Applications)

Multi-tenancy allows a **single Django application** to serve multiple **customers (tenants)** with **isolated data** while sharing the same codebase. This is crucial for **SaaS (Software as a Service) applications** like **Shopify, Slack, or Jira**, where each customer has a separate data space.

1.1 Multi-Tenant Models in Django

There are three main multi-tenancy approaches in Django:

1. **Shared Database with Tenant Filtering** (Single Database)
   - **All tenants share the same database** but are filtered by a tenant_id.
   - Example: **Django tenant filtering using foreign keys**.
2. **Schema-Based Multi-Tenancy** (PostgreSQL Schema Per Tenant)
   - Each tenant has a **separate database schema** but shares the same database instance.
   - Example: **Using django-tenants to manage schemas dynamically**.
3. **Database Per Tenant** (Separate Databases)
   - Each tenant has a **completely separate database**.
   - Example: **Using django-multitenant for tenant-aware models**.

1.2 Implementing Multi-Tenancy Using django-tenants (Schema-Based Approach)

The **schema-based approach** is ideal for **PostgreSQL-based SaaS platforms**, as it provides **data isolation without requiring multiple databases**.

273

Step 1: Install django-tenants

sh
CopyEdit
pip install django-tenants

Step 2: Configure Multi-Tenant Settings

Modify settings.py:

python
CopyEdit
```
DATABASES = {
    "default": {
        "ENGINE": "django_tenants.postgresql_backend",
        "NAME": "mydatabase",
        "USER": "myuser",
        "PASSWORD": "mypassword",
        "HOST": "localhost",
        "PORT": "5432",
    }
}

INSTALLED_APPS = [
    "django_tenants", # Multi-Tenant Support
    "customers", # Tenant-specific data
] + INSTALLED_APPS
```

■ **The database remains shared**, but each tenant gets a separate **schema**.

Step 3: Create the Tenant Model

Modify models.py in a customers app:

python
CopyEdit
```
from django_tenants.models import TenantMixin, DomainMixin
from django.db import models
```

```python
class Client(TenantMixin):
    name = models.CharField(max_length=100)
    created_on = models.DateTimeField(auto_now_add=True)

class Domain(DomainMixin):
    pass
```

■ Each **client (tenant)** has its **own schema**.

Step 4: Creating and Activating Tenants

Run migrations:

sh
CopyEdit
```sh
python manage.py migrate_schemas
```

Create a new tenant in shell:

python
CopyEdit
```python
from customers.models import Client, Domain

tenant = Client(schema_name="tenant1", name="Tenant 1")
tenant.save()

domain = Domain(domain="tenant1.myapp.com", tenant=tenant)
domain.save()
```

■ **Requests to** tenant1.myapp.com **are routed to that specific tenant's schema.**

Step 5: Middleware for Tenant Routing

Modify MIDDLEWARE in settings.py:

python
CopyEdit
```
MIDDLEWARE = [
    "django_tenants.middleware.main.TenantMainMiddleware",
] + MIDDLEWARE
```

■ **Django automatically detects the tenant from the domain name.**

1.3 Shared Database Multi-Tenancy (Row-Based Approach)

For **smaller SaaS platforms**, using a **tenant_id in models** is an alternative.

Modify models.py:

python
CopyEdit
```
class TenantModel(models.Model):
    tenant_id = models.UUIDField(default=uuid.uuid4, editable=False)

    class Meta:
        abstract = True

class Product(TenantModel):
    name = models.CharField(max_length=100)
    price = models.DecimalField(max_digits=10, decimal_places=2)
```

■ **Every query filters by** tenant_id to ensure data separation.

Django and GraphQL Integration

GraphQL is an alternative to **REST APIs**, offering: ■ **Flexible Queries** – Clients request **only the data they need**.
■ **Single Endpoint** – Reduces **over-fetching and under-fetching** of data.
■ **Better Performance** – Fetch **related data** in one request.

2.1 Installing GraphQL in Django

Django integrates GraphQL using **Graphene-Django**.

Step 1: Install Graphene-Django
sh
CopyEdit
```
pip install graphene-django
```

Add to INSTALLED_APPS in settings.py:

python
CopyEdit
```
INSTALLED_APPS += ["graphene_django"]
```

2.2 Defining a GraphQL Schema in Django

GraphQL requires defining **Types, Queries, and Mutations**.

Step 1: Create a GraphQL Type for a Model

Modify schema.py:

python
CopyEdit
```
import graphene
from graphene_django.types import DjangoObjectType
from .models import Product

class ProductType(DjangoObjectType):
    class Meta:
        model = Product
```

■ This maps the Product model to GraphQL.

Step 2: Define Queries (Fetching Data)

Modify schema.py:

python
CopyEdit
```python
class Query(graphene.ObjectType):
    all_products = graphene.List(ProductType)

    def resolve_all_products(self, info):
        return Product.objects.all()

schema = graphene.Schema(query=Query)
```

■ Now, GraphQL can fetch all products.

Step 3: Define Mutations (Creating and Updating Data)

Modify schema.py:

python
CopyEdit
```python
class CreateProduct(graphene.Mutation):
    class Arguments:
        name = graphene.String()
        price = graphene.Float()

    product = graphene.Field(ProductType)

    def mutate(self, info, name, price):
        product = Product(name=name, price=price)
        product.save()
        return CreateProduct(product=product)
```

278

```
class Mutation(graphene.ObjectType):
    create_product = CreateProduct.Field()

schema = graphene.Schema(query=Query, mutation=Mutation)
```

■ **Now, GraphQL can create new products.**

2.3 Exposing GraphQL Endpoint in Django

Modify urls.py:

python
CopyEdit
```
from django.urls import path
from graphene_django.views import GraphQLView
from .schema import schema

urlpatterns = [
    path("graphql/", GraphQLView.as_view(graphiql=True, schema=schema)),
]
```

■ **Visit** http://127.0.0.1:8000/graphql/ to interact with the GraphQL API.

2.4 Running GraphQL Queries and Mutations

Example Query: Fetch All Products

graphql
CopyEdit
```
{
  allProducts {
    name
    price
  }
}
```

279

Example Mutation: Create a New Product

graphql
CopyEdit

```
mutation {
 createProduct(name: "Laptop", price: 999.99) {
  product {
   name
   price
  }
 }
}
```

■ **GraphQL efficiently retrieves only the necessary data.**

■ **Multi-Tenant Architecture Enables SaaS Applications**

- Use django-tenants for **schema-based isolation**.
- Use tenant_id **filtering** for shared database approaches.

■ **GraphQL Enhances API Efficiency**

- Fetch **only required fields** using **Graphene-Django**.
- Reduce **over-fetching and under-fetching** of data.
- Support **real-time updates with GraphQL subscriptions** (WebSockets).

Django is not limited to traditional web applications. It can also serve as a **backend for Machine Learning (ML) and AI applications**, and it provides **internationalization (i18n) and localization (l10n) support** for creating multilingual web applications.

Using Django for Machine Learning and AI Applications

Django can integrate **machine learning models** built with **TensorFlow, PyTorch, or Scikit-Learn** to create **intelligent applications** like:

■ **Chatbots**

■ **Recommendation Systems**

- **Fraud Detection**
- **Image Recognition**

1.1 Deploying a Machine Learning Model in Django

Step 1: Train and Save a Model

Example: Train a **house price prediction model** using scikit-learn.

python

CopyEdit

```python
import pickle

from sklearn.linear_model import LinearRegression

import numpy as np


# Training Data (Example)

X = np.array([[1200], [1500], [1800], [2000], [2500]])

y = np.array([200000, 250000, 300000, 350000, 400000])


# Train Model

model = LinearRegression()

model.fit(X, y)


# Save Model to File

with open("ml_model.pkl", "wb") as file:

    pickle.dump(model, file)
```

■ **The model is now trained and saved as ml_model.pkl.**

Step 2: Load and Use the Model in Django

Modify views.py:

python

CopyEdit

```python
import pickle
import numpy as np
from django.http import JsonResponse


# Load the Model
with open("ml_model.pkl", "rb") as file:
    model = pickle.load(file)


def predict_price(request):
    try:
        size = float(request.GET.get("size", 1500))
        prediction = model.predict(np.array([[size]]))
        return JsonResponse({"predicted_price": prediction[0]})
    except Exception as e:
        return JsonResponse({"error": str(e)}, status=400)
```

■ Django now serves ML predictions via API.

Step 3: Expose ML Predictions as API Endpoint

Modify urls.py:

python

CopyEdit

```
from django.urls import path

from .views import predict_price


urlpatterns = [

    path("predict/", predict_price, name="predict"),

]
```

■ Visit http://127.0.0.1:8000/predict/?size=1800 to **get house price predictions**.

1.2 Integrating Django with TensorFlow for Deep Learning

If you are working with **deep learning models** (e.g., TensorFlow/Keras), follow the same approach:

python

CopyEdit

```
import tensorflow as tf


# Load Pretrained Model
```

283

```python
model = tf.keras.models.load_model("deep_learning_model.h5")


def classify_image(request):

    image = request.FILES["image"]

    image_data = preprocess_image(image)

    prediction = model.predict(image_data)

    return JsonResponse({"class": str(prediction.argmax())})
```

■ **Django can now classify images using deep learning**.

1.3 Using Django with NLP (Natural Language Processing)

Example: **Sentiment Analysis API** using transformers:

python

CopyEdit

```python
from transformers import pipeline

from django.http import JsonResponse


# Load Sentiment Analysis Model

sentiment_pipeline = pipeline("sentiment-analysis")


def analyze_sentiment(request):

    text = request.GET.get("text", "I love Django!")
```

284

```
result = sentiment_pipeline(text)

return JsonResponse(result[0])
```

■ **Django can now process text and return sentiment predictions.**

Implementing Multi-Language Support (i18n and l10n)

Internationalization (i18n) allows Django applications to **support multiple languages**, while **Localization (l10n)** adapts **formats (dates, currencies, numbers)** to specific regions.

■ Example: **A multilingual website supporting English, French, and Spanish.**

2.1 Enabling Django's i18n and l10n Features

Modify settings.py:

python

CopyEdit

```python
# Default Language

LANGUAGE_CODE = "en-us"


# Enable Internationalization

USE_I18N = True

USE_L10N = True

USE_TZ = True


# Supported Languages
```

```
LANGUAGES = [

   ("en", "English"),

   ("fr", "French"),

   ("es", "Spanish"),

]


# Translation Directory

LOCALE_PATHS = [

   BASE_DIR / "locale/",

]
```

■ **Django now recognizes multiple languages.**

2.2 Translating Django Templates

Modify base.html:

html

CopyEdit

```
{% load i18n %}
<html lang="{% get_current_language %}">
<head>
   <title>{% trans "Welcome to My Website" %}</title>
</head>
```

```
<body>
    <h1>{% trans "Hello, World!" %}</h1>
</body>
</html>
```

■ The {% trans %} tag makes text translatable.

2.3 Generating and Editing Translation Files

Step 1: Extract Translatable Strings

Run:

sh

CopyEdit

```
django-admin makemessages -l fr -l es
```

Django generates:

bash

CopyEdit

```
locale/
    ├── fr/LC_MESSAGES/django.po
    ├── es/LC_MESSAGES/django.po
```

287

Step 2: Edit Translation Files (django.po)

French (locale/fr/LC_MESSAGES/django.po):

po

CopyEdit

msgid "Hello, World!"

msgstr "Bonjour, le monde!"

Spanish (locale/es/LC_MESSAGES/django.po):

po

CopyEdit

msgid "Hello, World!"

msgstr "¡Hola, Mundo!"

2.4 Compiling Translations

Run:

sh

CopyEdit

django-admin compilemessages

■ **Django now serves translated content.**

288

2.5 Switching Languages in Views

Modify views.py:

python

CopyEdit

```python
from django.utils.translation import activate
from django.shortcuts import redirect


def switch_language(request, lang_code):
    activate(lang_code)
    return redirect("/")
```

Modify urls.py:

python

CopyEdit

```python
from django.urls import path
from .views import switch_language


urlpatterns = [
    path("lang/<str:lang_code>/", switch_language, name="switch_language"),
]
```

■ Users can switch languages dynamically.

289

2.6 Translating Django Forms and Models

Django also supports translations in **forms and models**.

Translating a Django Model

python

CopyEdit

```python
from django.utils.translation import gettext_lazy as _
from django.db import models


class Product(models.Model):
    name = models.CharField(_("Product Name"), max_length=255)
    description = models.TextField(_("Product Description"))
```

■ **Field labels are now translatable**.

2.7 Formatting Dates, Numbers, and Currencies

Django automatically **formats dates and numbers** based on **user locale**.

Modify views.py:

python

CopyEdit

```python
from django.utils import formats
from django.http import JsonResponse
import datetime
```

```
def localized_date(request):

    now = datetime.datetime.now()

    return JsonResponse({"date": formats.date_format(now,
"SHORT_DATE_FORMAT")})
```

■ **Django adjusts date formatting per locale.**

■ **Django Supports Machine Learning and AI**

- Load **Scikit-Learn, TensorFlow, and NLP models** into Django APIs.
- Serve **predictions via REST endpoints.**

■ **GraphQL Enhances API Efficiency**

- Fetch **only required fields** using **Graphene-Django.**
- Reduce **over-fetching and under-fetching** of data.
- Support **real-time updates with GraphQL subscriptions** (WebSockets).

■ **Django Provides Full Multi-Language Support**

- Translate **templates, models, and forms** using **gettext.**
- Switch **languages dynamically** in views.
- Format **dates and currencies** based on locale.

By implementing **Machine Learning, GraphQL, and i18n/l10n**, Django applications become **more intelligent, efficient, and accessible to a global audience.**

Chapter 14: Real-World Django Projects (Hands-On)

Project 1: Blogging Platform with User Authentication

Project Overview

This blogging platform will include:
- **User Authentication** – Register, login, logout, and profile management.
- **Blog Post Management** – Create, edit, delete, and list blog posts.
- **Categories and Tags** – Organize blog posts into different topics.
- **Comment System** – Allow users to leave comments on posts.

1. Setting Up the Django Blogging Project

Step 1: Create a Django Project

Run the following command:

sh
CopyEdit
```
django-admin startproject blog_project
cd blog_project
```

Step 2: Create the Blog App

Inside the project folder, create a new app:

sh
CopyEdit
```
python manage.py startapp blog
```

Add blog to INSTALLED_APPS in settings.py:

python
CopyEdit
```
INSTALLED_APPS += ["blog"]
```
292

■ Django is now ready to handle blog-related functionality.

2. User Registration, Login, and Profile Management

Step 1: Set Up Django's Built-in Authentication

Modify settings.py to use Django's authentication system:

python
CopyEdit
```python
AUTHENTICATION_BACKENDS = ["django.contrib.auth.backends.ModelBackend"]
LOGIN_REDIRECT_URL = "home"
LOGOUT_REDIRECT_URL = "login"
```

Step 2: Create User Registration View

Modify forms.py inside blog app:

python
CopyEdit
```python
from django import forms
from django.contrib.auth.models import User

class UserRegistrationForm(forms.ModelForm):
    password = forms.CharField(widget=forms.PasswordInput)

    class Meta:
        model = User
        fields = ["username", "email", "password"]
```

Modify views.py:

python
CopyEdit
```python
from django.shortcuts import render, redirect
from .forms import UserRegistrationForm
from django.contrib.auth import login

def register(request):
```

293

```python
if request.method == "POST":
    form = UserRegistrationForm(request.POST)
    if form.is_valid():
        user = form.save(commit=False)
        user.set_password(form.cleaned_data["password"])
        user.save()
        login(request, user)
        return redirect("home")
    else:
        form = UserRegistrationForm()
    return render(request, "blog/register.html", {"form": form})
```

■ **Users can now register.**

Step 3: Implement Login and Logout

Modify urls.py:

python
CopyEdit
```python
from django.contrib.auth.views import LoginView, LogoutView
from .views import register

urlpatterns = [
    path("register/", register, name="register"),
    path("login/", LoginView.as_view(template_name="blog/login.html"),
name="login"),
    path("logout/", LogoutView.as_view(), name="logout"),
]
```

■ **Django's authentication system is fully functional.**

Step 4: User Profile Management

Modify models.py to extend the User model:

python
CopyEdit

```
from django.db import models
from django.contrib.auth.models import User

class Profile(models.Model):
    user = models.OneToOneField(User, on_delete=models.CASCADE)
    bio = models.TextField(blank=True)
    avatar = models.ImageField(upload_to="avatars/", default="default.jpg")

    def __str__(self):
        return f"{self.user.username} Profile"
```

■ **Each user now has a profile.**

3. CRUD Functionality for Blog Posts

Step 1: Create the Blog Model

Modify models.py:

python
CopyEdit

```
class BlogPost(models.Model):
    title = models.CharField(max_length=200)
    content = models.TextField()
    author = models.ForeignKey(User, on_delete=models.CASCADE)
    created_at = models.DateTimeField(auto_now_add=True)
    updated_at = models.DateTimeField(auto_now=True)

    def __str__(self):
        return self.title
```

295

Run migrations:

sh
CopyEdit
```
python manage.py makemigrations
python manage.py migrate
```

■ **Django now tracks blog posts.**

Step 2: Implement CRUD Views for Blog Posts

Modify views.py:

python
CopyEdit
```python
from django.shortcuts import render, get_object_or_404, redirect
from .models import BlogPost
from django.contrib.auth.decorators import login_required

@login_required
def create_post(request):
    if request.method == "POST":
        title = request.POST["title"]
        content = request.POST["content"]
        BlogPost.objects.create(title=title, content=content, author=request.user)
        return redirect("home")
    return render(request, "blog/create_post.html")

def post_list(request):
    posts = BlogPost.objects.all().order_by("-created_at")
    return render(request, "blog/post_list.html", {"posts": posts})

def post_detail(request, pk):
    post = get_object_or_404(BlogPost, pk=pk)
    return render(request, "blog/post_detail.html", {"post": post})

@login_required
```

```python
def update_post(request, pk):
    post = get_object_or_404(BlogPost, pk=pk, author=request.user)
    if request.method == "POST":
        post.title = request.POST["title"]
        post.content = request.POST["content"]
        post.save()
        return redirect("post_detail", pk=pk)
    return render(request, "blog/update_post.html", {"post": post})

@login_required
def delete_post(request, pk):
    post = get_object_or_404(BlogPost, pk=pk, author=request.user)
    if request.method == "POST":
        post.delete()
        return redirect("home")
    return render(request, "blog/delete_post.html", {"post": post})
```

■ **Users can now create, read, update, and delete blog posts.**

Step 3: Add Blog URLs

Modify urls.py:

python
CopyEdit
```python
from django.urls import path
from .views import create_post, post_list, post_detail, update_post, delete_post

urlpatterns = [
    path("", post_list, name="home"),
    path("post/<int:pk>/", post_detail, name="post_detail"),
    path("post/new/", create_post, name="create_post"),
    path("post/<int:pk>/edit/", update_post, name="update_post"),
    path("post/<int:pk>/delete/", delete_post, name="delete_post"),
]
```

■ **Django now routes blog requests correctly.**

4. Implementing Categories, Tags, and Comments

Step 1: Add Categories and Tags to the Blog Model

Modify models.py:

python
CopyEdit
```python
class Category(models.Model):
    name = models.CharField(max_length=100, unique=True)

class Tag(models.Model):
    name = models.CharField(max_length=100, unique=True)

class BlogPost(models.Model):
    title = models.CharField(max_length=200)
    content = models.TextField()
    author = models.ForeignKey(User, on_delete=models.CASCADE)
    categories = models.ManyToManyField(Category)
    tags = models.ManyToManyField(Tag)
```

Run migrations:

sh
CopyEdit
```sh
python manage.py makemigrations
python manage.py migrate
```

■ **Blog posts now support categories and tags.**

Step 2: Implement a Comment System

Modify models.py:

python
CopyEdit
```
class Comment(models.Model):
    post = models.ForeignKey(BlogPost, on_delete=models.CASCADE,
related_name="comments")
    author = models.ForeignKey(User, on_delete=models.CASCADE)
    text = models.TextField()
    created_at = models.DateTimeField(auto_now_add=True)
```

Modify views.py:

python
CopyEdit
```
@login_required
def add_comment(request, pk):
    post = get_object_or_404(BlogPost, pk=pk)
    if request.method == "POST":
        text = request.POST["text"]
        Comment.objects.create(post=post, author=request.user, text=text)
    return redirect("post_detail", pk=pk)
```

■ **Users can now comment on blog posts.**

■ **User Authentication** – Users can register, log in, and manage profiles.
■ **CRUD for Blog Posts** – Users can **create, edit, delete, and list** blog posts.
■ **Categories & Tags** – Organize blog posts into structured topics.
■ **Comment System** – Users can interact via **comments on posts**.

Project 2: E-Commerce Store with Payment Gateway

An e-commerce store requires multiple features, including **product listings, a shopping cart, checkout functionality, and payment gateway integration**. This hands-on project will guide you through **building a Django-based e-commerce platform** with **Stripe and PayPal** as payment gateways.

Project Overview

This e-commerce platform will include:
■ **Product Listings and Categories** – Display products with search and filter functionality.
■ **Shopping Cart and Checkout** – Allow users to add/remove products and proceed to checkout.
■ **Payment Gateway Integration** – Accept payments using **Stripe and PayPal**.

1. Setting Up the E-Commerce Project

Step 1: Create a Django Project and App

Run the following command:

sh
CopyEdit
```
django-admin startproject ecommerce_project
cd ecommerce_project
python manage.py startapp store
```

Add store to INSTALLED_APPS in settings.py:

python
CopyEdit
```
INSTALLED_APPS += ["store"]
```

■ **Django is now ready for e-commerce features.**

2. Product Listings and Categories

Step 1: Define the Product and Category Models

Modify models.py inside the store app:

python
CopyEdit
```python
from django.db import models

class Category(models.Model):
    name = models.CharField(max_length=255, unique=True)
    slug = models.SlugField(unique=True)

    def __str__(self):
        return self.name

class Product(models.Model):
    name = models.CharField(max_length=255)
    description = models.TextField()
    price = models.DecimalField(max_digits=10, decimal_places=2)
    category = models.ForeignKey(Category, on_delete=models.CASCADE)
    image = models.ImageField(upload_to="product_images/")
    stock = models.PositiveIntegerField(default=0)
    created_at = models.DateTimeField(auto_now_add=True)

    def __str__(self):
        return self.name
```

Run migrations:

sh
CopyEdit
```sh
python manage.py makemigrations store
python manage.py migrate
```

■ **Products and categories are now stored in the database.**

Step 2: Implement Product Listing Views

Modify views.py:

python
CopyEdit
```
from django.shortcuts import render, get_object_or_404
from .models import Product, Category

def product_list(request):
    products = Product.objects.all()
    categories = Category.objects.all()
    return render(request, "store/product_list.html", {"products": products, "categories":
categories})

def product_detail(request, product_id):
    product = get_object_or_404(Product, id=product_id)
    return render(request, "store/product_detail.html", {"product": product})
```

■ **Users can browse products and categories.**

Step 3: Add Product URLs

Modify urls.py:

python
CopyEdit
```
from django.urls import path
from .views import product_list, product_detail

urlpatterns = [
    path("", product_list, name="product_list"),
    path("product/<int:product_id>/", product_detail, name="product_detail"),
]
```

■ **Django now routes product requests correctly.**

302

3. Implementing Shopping Cart and Checkout

Step 1: Create a Cart System

Modify models.py:

python
CopyEdit
```python
from django.contrib.auth.models import User

class CartItem(models.Model):
    user = models.ForeignKey(User, on_delete=models.CASCADE)
    product = models.ForeignKey(Product, on_delete=models.CASCADE)
    quantity = models.PositiveIntegerField(default=1)

    def total_price(self):
        return self.product.price * self.quantity
```

■ **The cart stores user-selected products.**

Step 2: Implement Add/Remove Cart Views

Modify views.py:

python
CopyEdit
```python
from django.shortcuts import redirect
from .models import CartItem, Product

def add_to_cart(request, product_id):
    product = Product.objects.get(id=product_id)
    cart_item, created = CartItem.objects.get_or_create(user=request.user,
product=product)
    cart_item.quantity += 1
    cart_item.save()
    return redirect("cart_view")

def remove_from_cart(request, cart_item_id):
    cart_item = CartItem.objects.get(id=cart_item_id, user=request.user)
```

```
    cart_item.delete()
    return redirect("cart_view")

def cart_view(request):
    cart_items = CartItem.objects.filter(user=request.user)
    total = sum(item.total_price() for item in cart_items)
    return render(request, "store/cart.html", {"cart_items": cart_items, "total": total})
```

■ Users can now add/remove products from the cart.

Step 3: Implement Checkout

Modify views.py:

python
CopyEdit
```
from django.contrib.auth.decorators import login_required
from django.shortcuts import render

@login_required
def checkout(request):
    cart_items = CartItem.objects.filter(user=request.user)
    total = sum(item.total_price() for item in cart_items)
    return render(request, "store/checkout.html", {"cart_items": cart_items, "total": total})
```

■ Users can proceed to checkout before making a payment.

Step 4: Add Shopping Cart URLs

Modify urls.py:

python
CopyEdit
```
from .views import add_to_cart, remove_from_cart, cart_view, checkout
```

```
urlpatterns += [
    path("cart/", cart_view, name="cart_view"),
    path("cart/add/<int:product_id>/", add_to_cart, name="add_to_cart"),
    path("cart/remove/<int:cart_item_id>/", remove_from_cart,
name="remove_from_cart"),
    path("checkout/", checkout, name="checkout"),
]
```

■ **The cart and checkout functionalities are now accessible.**

4. Integrating Payment Gateways (Stripe, PayPal)

4.1 Integrating Stripe Payment

Step 1: Install Stripe
sh
CopyEdit
```
pip install stripe
```

Step 2: Configure Stripe API Keys in settings.py
python
CopyEdit
```
STRIPE_PUBLIC_KEY = "your_stripe_public_key"
STRIPE_SECRET_KEY = "your_stripe_secret_key"
```

Step 3: Create Payment View in views.py
python
CopyEdit
```
import stripe
from django.conf import settings
from django.http import JsonResponse

stripe.api_key = settings.STRIPE_SECRET_KEY

def stripe_checkout(request):
```

```
try:
    checkout_session = stripe.checkout.Session.create(
        payment_method_types=["card"],
        line_items=[
            {
                "price_data": {
                    "currency": "usd",
                    "product_data": {"name": "E-Commerce Order"},
                    "unit_amount": int(request.GET.get("amount")) * 100,
                },
                "quantity": 1,
            }
        ],
        mode="payment",
        success_url="http://127.0.0.1:8000/payment-success/",
        cancel_url="http://127.0.0.1:8000/payment-failed/",
    )
    return JsonResponse({"id": checkout_session.id})
except Exception as e:
    return JsonResponse({"error": str(e)}, status=400)
```

█ **Stripe processes payments securely.**

4.2 Integrating PayPal Payment

Step 1: Install paypalrestsdk
sh
CopyEdit

```
pip install paypalrestsdk
```

Step 2: Configure PayPal in settings.py
python
CopyEdit

```
PAYPAL_CLIENT_ID = "your_paypal_client_id"
PAYPAL_SECRET = "your_paypal_secret_key"
```

306

Step 3: Implement PayPal Payment View
python
CopyEdit
```python
import paypalrestsdk
from django.conf import settings

paypalrestsdk.configure({
    "mode": "sandbox",
    "client_id": settings.PAYPAL_CLIENT_ID,
    "client_secret": settings.PAYPAL_SECRET,
})

def paypal_checkout(request):
    payment = paypalrestsdk.Payment({
        "intent": "sale",
        "payer": {"payment_method": "paypal"},
        "redirect_urls": {
            "return_url": "http://127.0.0.1:8000/payment-success/",
            "cancel_url": "http://127.0.0.1:8000/payment-failed/",
        },
        "transactions": [{"amount": {"total": "10.00", "currency": "USD"}}]
    })
    if payment.create():
        return JsonResponse({"approval_url": payment["links"][1]["href"]})
    return JsonResponse({"error": "Payment failed."}, status=400)
```

■ **PayPal provides another payment option.**

■ **E-Commerce Features** – Users can browse, add products to cart, and checkout.
■ **Stripe & PayPal Integration** – Accept secure online payments.
■ **Django Handles Order Processing** – Ensures smooth transactions.

Project 3: Social Media App with WebSockets

A social media application requires **real-time updates, user interactions**, and **live messaging**. This project will use **Django Channels and WebSockets** to enable **real-time chat, friend requests, notifications, and activity feeds**.

Project Overview

This social media platform will include:
■ **User Profiles** – Users can edit their profiles, upload avatars, and manage friend requests.
■ **Real-Time Chat with WebSockets** – Users can send instant messages using **Django Channels**.
■ **Notifications and Activity Feeds** – Users get notified of **friend requests, likes, and messages**.

1. Setting Up the Django Social Media Project

Step 1: Create a Django Project and App

sh

CopyEdit

```
django-admin startproject social_media_project
cd social_media_project
python manage.py startapp social
```

Add social to INSTALLED_APPS in settings.py:

python

CopyEdit

```
INSTALLED_APPS += ["social", "channels"]
```

■ Django Channels will enable real-time WebSockets communication.

Step 2: Install Django Channels for WebSockets

sh

CopyEdit

```
pip install channels
```

Modify settings.py:

python

CopyEdit

```
ASGI_APPLICATION = "social_media_project.asgi.application"

CHANNEL_LAYERS = {
    "default": {
        "BACKEND": "channels.layers.InMemoryChannelLayer",
    }
}
```

■ Django is now configured to handle real-time WebSockets.

2. User Profiles, Friend Requests, and Messaging

Step 1: Create User Profile Model

Modify models.py:

python

CopyEdit

```python
from django.db import models
from django.contrib.auth.models import User


class Profile(models.Model):
    user = models.OneToOneField(User, on_delete=models.CASCADE)
    avatar = models.ImageField(upload_to="avatars/", default="default.jpg")
    bio = models.TextField(blank=True)
    friends = models.ManyToManyField("self", blank=True)

    def __str__(self):
        return self.user.username
```

■ Each user has a profile and a list of friends.

Step 2: Friend Request System

Modify models.py:

python

CopyEdit

```python
class FriendRequest(models.Model):

    from_user = models.ForeignKey(User, related_name="sent_requests", on_delete=models.CASCADE)

    to_user = models.ForeignKey(User, related_name="received_requests", on_delete=models.CASCADE)

    timestamp = models.DateTimeField(auto_now_add=True)
```

■ **Users can send and receive friend requests.**

Step 3: Friend Request Views

Modify views.py:

python

CopyEdit

```python
from django.shortcuts import get_object_or_404, redirect

from .models import Profile, FriendRequest


def send_friend_request(request, user_id):

    to_user = get_object_or_404(User, id=user_id)

    FriendRequest.objects.create(from_user=request.user, to_user=to_user)
```

311

```python
return redirect("profile", user_id=user_id)


def accept_friend_request(request, request_id):
    friend_request = get_object_or_404(FriendRequest, id=request_id)
    friend_request.to_user.profile.friends.add(friend_request.from_user)
    friend_request.from_user.profile.friends.add(friend_request.to_user)
    friend_request.delete()
    return redirect("profile", user_id=friend_request.to_user.id)
```

■ **Users can send and accept friend requests.**

3. Implementing WebSockets for Real-Time Chat

Step 1: Create Chat Model

Modify models.py:

python

CopyEdit

```python
class Message(models.Model):
    sender = models.ForeignKey(User, on_delete=models.CASCADE,
    related_name="sent_messages")

    receiver = models.ForeignKey(User, on_delete=models.CASCADE,
    related_name="received_messages")

    text = models.TextField()

    timestamp = models.DateTimeField(auto_now_add=True)
```

■ **Messages are stored in the database.**

Step 2: Set Up Django Channels WebSocket Routing

Modify routing.py:

python

CopyEdit

```python
from django.urls import path
from .consumers import ChatConsumer

websocket_urlpatterns = [
    path("ws/chat/<str:username>/", ChatConsumer.as_asgi()),
]
```

Modify asgi.py:

python

CopyEdit

```python
from channels.routing import ProtocolTypeRouter, URLRouter
from channels.auth import AuthMiddlewareStack
import social.routing

application = ProtocolTypeRouter({
```

313

```python
    "http": get_asgi_application(),

    "websocket":
AuthMiddlewareStack(URLRouter(social.routing.websocket_urlpatterns)),

})
```

■ **WebSockets are now handled in Django Channels.**

Step 3: Create WebSocket Consumer for Chat

Modify consumers.py:

python

CopyEdit

```python
import json
from channels.generic.websocket import AsyncWebsocketConsumer


class ChatConsumer(AsyncWebsocketConsumer):
    async def connect(self):
        self.room_name = self.scope["url_route"]["kwargs"]["username"]
        self.room_group_name = f"chat_{self.room_name}"

        await self.channel_layer.group_add(self.room_group_name, self.channel_name)
        await self.accept()

    async def disconnect(self, close_code):
```

314

```python
        await self.channel_layer.group_discard(self.room_group_name, self.channel_name)

    async def receive(self, text_data):
        data = json.loads(text_data)
        message = data["message"]
        sender = self.scope["user"].username

        await self.channel_layer.group_send(
            self.room_group_name,
            {
                "type": "chat_message",
                "message": message,
                "sender": sender,
            }
        )

    async def chat_message(self, self, event):
        await self.send(text_data=json.dumps(event))
```

■ **Real-time chat is now functional using WebSockets.**

Step 4: Create Chat View and URL

Modify views.py:

python

CopyEdit

```
from django.shortcuts import render


def chat_view(request, username):
    return render(request, "social/chat.html", {"username": username})
```

Modify urls.py:

python

CopyEdit

```
urlpatterns += [
    path("chat/<str:username>/", chat_view, name="chat"),
]
```

■ **Users can now access chat rooms via WebSockets.**

4. Notifications and Activity Feeds

Step 1: Create Notification Model

Modify models.py:

python

CopyEdit

```python
class Notification(models.Model):
    user = models.ForeignKey(User, on_delete=models.CASCADE)
    message = models.TextField()
    is_read = models.BooleanField(default=False)
    timestamp = models.DateTimeField(auto_now_add=True)
```

◼ **Users receive notifications when new messages or friend requests arrive.**

Step 2: Display Notifications

Modify views.py:

python

CopyEdit

```python
def notifications(request):
    notifications = Notification.objects.filter(user=request.user, is_read=False)
    return render(request, "social/notifications.html", {"notifications": notifications})
```

◼ **Users can check unread notifications.**

317

Step 3: Notify Users in Real-Time

Modify consumers.py:

python

CopyEdit

```python
async def receive(self, text_data):
    data = json.loads(text_data)
    message = data["message"]
    sender = self.scope["user"].username

    await Notification.objects.create(
        user=self.scope["user"],
        message=f"New message from {sender}: {message}",
    )

    await self.channel_layer.group_send(
        self.room_group_name,
        {"type": "chat_message", "message": message, "sender": sender}
    )
```

■ **Users receive real-time notifications.**

318

Django Channels Enables Real-Time Chat – WebSockets allow **instant messaging**.
Friend Requests Create a Social Experience – Users can **connect and build relationships**.
Activity Feeds and Notifications Enhance Engagement – Users stay **updated in real time**.

This **social media project** demonstrates how Django can power a **modern, real-time web application**

Project 4: Task Management API with Django REST Framework

A task management system is essential for project tracking and workflow organization. This project will focus on building a RESTful API for managing tasks with authentication, permissions, and a frontend dashboard.

Project Overview

This task management system will include:
User-Based Task Assignment and Status Updates – Users can create, assign, and update tasks.
API Authentication and Permissions – Secure API endpoints with JWT authentication.
Building a Frontend Dashboard – Create a simple dashboard to interact with the API.

1. Setting Up the Django Task Management Project

Step 1: Create a Django Project and App

sh

CopyEdit

```
django-admin startproject task_project
```

319

```
cd task_project

python manage.py startapp tasks
```

Add tasks **and** rest_framework **to** INSTALLED_APPS **in** settings.py**:**

python

CopyEdit

```
INSTALLED_APPS += ["tasks", "rest_framework",
"rest_framework_simplejwt"]
```

■ **Django is now ready to handle REST API requests.**

2. User-Based Task Assignment and Status Updates

Step 1: Define the Task Model

Modify models.py **inside the** tasks **app:**

python

CopyEdit

```
from django.db import models

from django.contrib.auth.models import User


class Task(models.Model):
    STATUS_CHOICES = [
        ("pending", "Pending"),
        ("in_progress", "In Progress"),
```

320

```python
    ("completed", "Completed"),
]


title = models.CharField(max_length=255)

description = models.TextField()

assigned_to = models.ForeignKey(User, on_delete=models.CASCADE)

status = models.CharField(max_length=20, choices=STATUS_CHOICES, default="pending")

created_at = models.DateTimeField(auto_now_add=True)

updated_at = models.DateTimeField(auto_now=True)


def __str__(self):

    return self.title
```

Run migrations:

sh

CopyEdit

python manage.py makemigrations tasks

python manage.py migrate

■ Tasks now track assignments and status updates.

Step 2: Create Serializers for Task API

Modify serializers.py:

python

CopyEdit

```
from rest_framework import serializers
from .models import Task


class TaskSerializer(serializers.ModelSerializer):
    class Meta:
        model = Task
        fields = "__all__"
```

■ Django REST Framework now serializes Task data.

Step 3: Implement Task API Views

Modify views.py:

python

CopyEdit

```
from rest_framework import generics
from rest_framework.permissions import IsAuthenticated
from .models import Task
from .serializers import TaskSerializer
```

```python
class TaskListCreateView(generics.ListCreateAPIView):
    queryset = Task.objects.all()
    serializer_class = TaskSerializer
    permission_classes = [IsAuthenticated]

    def perform_create(self, serializer):
        serializer.save(assigned_to=self.request.user)


class TaskRetrieveUpdateDeleteView(generics.RetrieveUpdateDestroyAPIView):
    queryset = Task.objects.all()
    serializer_class = TaskSerializer
    permission_classes = [IsAuthenticated]
```

■ **Users can now create, read, update, and delete tasks via API.**

Step 4: Configure API URLs

Modify urls.py:

python

CopyEdit

```python
from django.urls import path
from .views import TaskListCreateView, TaskRetrieveUpdateDeleteView
```

```python
urlpatterns = [

    path("tasks/", TaskListCreateView.as_view(), name="task_list"),

    path("tasks/<int:pk>/", TaskRetrieveUpdateDeleteView.as_view(),
name="task_detail"),

]
```

■ Django REST Framework now exposes API endpoints.

3. API Authentication and Permissions

Step 1: Enable JWT Authentication

Modify settings.py:

python

CopyEdit

```python
from datetime import timedelta


REST_FRAMEWORK = {
    "DEFAULT_AUTHENTICATION_CLASSES": [
        "rest_framework_simplejwt.authentication.JWTAuthentication",
    ],
    "DEFAULT_PERMISSION_CLASSES": [
        "rest_framework.permissions.IsAuthenticated",
    ],
```

324

}

SIMPLE_JWT = {

  "ACCESS_TOKEN_LIFETIME": timedelta(days=1),

}

■ **Users must authenticate via JWT tokens.**

Step 2: Add Authentication URLs

Modify urls.py **in** task_project:

python

CopyEdit

from django.urls import path

from rest_framework_simplejwt.views import TokenObtainPairView, TokenRefreshView

urlpatterns = [

  path("api/token/", TokenObtainPairView.as_view(), name="token_obtain_pair"),

  path("api/token/refresh/", TokenRefreshView.as_view(), name="token_refresh"),

]

■ **Users can obtain and refresh authentication tokens.**

Step 3: Implement Task Permissions

Modify permissions.py:

python

CopyEdit

```python
from rest_framework.permissions import BasePermission


class IsTaskOwner(BasePermission):
    def has_object_permission(self, request, view, obj):
        return obj.assigned_to == request.user
```

Modify views.py:

python

CopyEdit

```python
from .permissions import IsTaskOwner


class TaskRetrieveUpdateDeleteView(generics.RetrieveUpdateDestroyAPIView):
    queryset = Task.objects.all()
    serializer_class = TaskSerializer
    permission_classes = [IsAuthenticated, IsTaskOwner]
```

■ **Only task owners can modify their tasks.**

326

4. Building a Frontend Dashboard

Step 1: Set Up React for the Frontend

Inside the Django project, create a React app:

sh

CopyEdit

```sh
npx create-react-app frontend
cd frontend
npm start
```

■ The frontend will consume the Django API.

Step 2: Fetch Tasks from API

Modify App.js in React:

jsx

CopyEdit

```jsx
import React, { useState, useEffect } from "react";

const API_URL = "http://127.0.0.1:8000/tasks/";

function App() {
  const [tasks, setTasks] = useState([]);
```

```
useEffect(() => {
  fetch(API_URL, {
    headers: {
      Authorization: `Bearer ${localStorage.getItem("access_token")}`,
    },
  })
    .then((response) => response.json())
    .then((data) => setTasks(data));
}, []);

return (
  <div>
    <h1>Task Management Dashboard</h1>
    <ul>
      {tasks.map((task) => (
        <li key={task.id}>{task.title} - {task.status}</li>
      ))}
    </ul>
  </div>
);
}
```

export default App;

■ The dashboard displays tasks retrieved from the Django API.

Step 3: Implement Login and Token Storage

Modify Login.js:

jsx

CopyEdit

```jsx
import React, { useState } from "react";

const LOGIN_URL = "http://127.0.0.1:8000/api/token/";

function Login() {
  const [username, setUsername] = useState("");
  const [password, setPassword] = useState("");

  const handleLogin = async (e) => {
    e.preventDefault();
    const response = await fetch(LOGIN_URL, {
      method: "POST",
      headers: { "Content-Type": "application/json" },
      body: JSON.stringify({ username, password }),
```

329

```
    });

    const data = await response.json();

    localStorage.setItem("access_token", data.access);

    window.location.href = "/";

  };


  return (

   <form onSubmit={handleLogin}>

     <input type="text" placeholder="Username" onChange={(e) =>
setUsername(e.target.value)} />

     <input type="password" placeholder="Password" onChange={(e) =>
setPassword(e.target.value)} />

     <button type="submit">Login</button>

   </form>

  );

}


export default Login;
```

■ Users can now log in and receive authentication tokens.

Project 5: AI-Powered Django App

Artificial Intelligence (AI) is transforming how applications operate. By integrating AI models with Django, we can create intelligent applications for image recognition, chatbots, and natural language processing (NLP) using OpenAI's GPT, TensorFlow, or other AI frameworks.

Project Overview

This AI-powered Django app will include:
■ **Integrating OpenAI or TensorFlow for AI Features** – Implement AI models inside Django.
■ **Real-World Use Cases** – Create an Image Recognition App, an NLP-powered Chatbot, or a Text Summarizer.

1. Setting Up the AI-Powered Django Project

Step 1: Create a Django Project and App

sh

CopyEdit

```
django-admin startproject ai_project

cd ai_project

python manage.py startapp ai_app
```

Add ai_app **to** INSTALLED_APPS **in** settings.py:

python

CopyEdit

```
INSTALLED_APPS += ["ai_app"]
```

■ **Django is now ready for AI integration.**

2. Integrating OpenAI or TensorFlow for AI Features

Option 1: Using OpenAI's GPT for NLP (Chatbots, Summarization, Text Analysis)

Step 1: Install OpenAI API SDK

sh

CopyEdit

```
pip install openai
```

Step 2: Configure OpenAI API Key in settings.py

python

CopyEdit

```
OPENAI_API_KEY = "your_openai_api_key"
```

Step 3: Implement AI-Powered Text Processing (Chatbot, Summarization, Sentiment Analysis)

Modify views.py**:**

python

CopyEdit

```
import openai

from django.conf import settings

from django.http import JsonResponse
```

```python
openai.api_key = settings.OPENAI_API_KEY


def ai_chatbot(request):

    user_input = request.GET.get("text", "Hello!")


    response = openai.ChatCompletion.create(

        model="gpt-3.5-turbo",

        messages=[{"role": "user", "content": user_input}],

    )


    return JsonResponse({"response":
response["choices"][0]["message"]["content"]})
```

■ This endpoint allows users to chat with an AI chatbot using GPT.

Option 2: Using TensorFlow for Image Recognition

Step 1: Install TensorFlow and Pillow (for image processing)

sh

CopyEdit

```
pip install tensorflow pillow
```

Step 2: Implement an AI-Powered Image Classifier

Modify views.py:

python

CopyEdit

```
import tensorflow as tf

import numpy as np

from django.core.files.storage import default_storage

from django.http import JsonResponse

from PIL import Image


# Load a pre-trained AI model

model = tf.keras.applications.MobileNetV2(weights="imagenet")


def classify_image(request):

    image_file = request.FILES["image"]

    image_path = default_storage.save("temp.jpg", image_file)


    image = Image.open(image_path).resize((224, 224))

    image_array = np.array(image) / 255.0

    image_array = np.expand_dims(image_array, axis=0)


    predictions = model.predict(image_array)
```

```
predicted_label =
tf.keras.applications.mobilenet_v2.decode_predictions(predictions, top=1)[0][0][1]


return JsonResponse({"prediction": predicted_label})
```

■ Users can now upload an image, and the AI model will classify it.

3. Real-World Use Cases

Use Case 1: Building an AI-Powered Chatbot

1. Users input a message.
2. GPT processes the request and generates a response.
3. Django returns the AI-generated response to the user.

Modify urls.py:

python

CopyEdit

```python
from django.urls import path

from .views import ai_chatbot


urlpatterns = [

    path("chatbot/", ai_chatbot, name="ai_chatbot"),

]
```


■ Now, users can chat with an AI assistant using Django.

335

Use Case 2: AI-Powered Text Summarization

Modify views.py:

python

CopyEdit

```python
def summarize_text(request):
    text = request.GET.get("text", "Django is a powerful web framework...")


    response = openai.ChatCompletion.create(
        model="gpt-3.5-turbo",
        messages=[{"role": "user", "content": f"Summarize this: {text}"}],
    )


    return JsonResponse({"summary": response["choices"][0]["message"]["content"]})
```

■ Users can submit a long text and receive a summarized version.

Use Case 3: AI-Powered Sentiment Analysis

Modify views.py:

python

CopyEdit

```python
def analyze_sentiment(request):
    text = request.GET.get("text", "I love Django!")
```

```python
response = openai.ChatCompletion.create(

    model="gpt-3.5-turbo",

    messages=[{"role": "user", "content": f"Analyze sentiment: {text}"}],

)


    return JsonResponse({"sentiment":
response["choices"][0]["message"]["content"]})
```

■ Users can analyze the sentiment of any text.

4. Creating a Frontend for AI Features

Step 1: Set Up React for AI Integration

Inside the Django project, create a React frontend:

sh

CopyEdit

```sh
npx create-react-app frontend

cd frontend

npm start
```

■ The frontend will communicate with Django's AI-powered API.

Step 2: Create a Chatbot Interface

Modify Chatbot.js:

jsx

CopyEdit

```jsx
import React, { useState } from "react";

const API_URL = "http://127.0.0.1:8000/chatbot/";

function Chatbot() {
  const [message, setMessage] = useState("");
  const [response, setResponse] = useState("");

  const sendMessage = async () => {
    const res = await fetch(`${API_URL}?text=${message}`);
    const data = await res.json();
    setResponse(data.response);
  };

  return (
    <div>
      <h1>AI Chatbot</h1>
      <input type="text" onChange={(e) => setMessage(e.target.value)} />
```

```jsx
        <button onClick={sendMessage}>Send</button>

        <p>{response}</p>

      </div>

  );

}


export default Chatbot;
```

■ **Users can now chat with an AI-powered assistant.**

Step 3: Create an Image Classification Interface

Modify ImageUpload.js:

jsx

CopyEdit

```jsx
import React, { useState } from "react";


const API_URL = "http://127.0.0.1:8000/classify/";


function ImageUpload() {

  const [image, setImage] = useState(null);

  const [prediction, setPrediction] = useState("");
```

```
const handleUpload = async () => {

  const formData = new FormData();

  formData.append("image", image);


  const res = await fetch(API_URL, {

    method: "POST",

    body: formData,

  });


  const data = await res.json();

  setPrediction(data.prediction);

};


return (

  <div>

    <h1>Image Classifier</h1>

    <input type="file" onChange={(e) => setImage(e.target.files[0])} />

    <button onClick={handleUpload}>Upload</button>

    <p>{prediction}</p>

  </div>

);

}
```

export default ImageUpload;

■ Users can upload images and get AI-based classifications.

Chapter 15: Django Performance Optimization and Scalability

Performance optimization is critical for **scaling Django applications**. Without proper optimization, Django apps can experience **slow database queries, inefficient caching, and unnecessary resource usage**.

Query Optimization and Database Indexing

1.1 Understanding Django ORM Queries

Django's ORM (Object-Relational Mapping) simplifies database queries but can generate **inefficient SQL statements** if not handled correctly.

■ **Optimizing queries ensures that the database handles large datasets efficiently.**

1.2 Identifying Slow Queries with django-debug-toolbar

The django-debug-toolbar helps analyze **query execution time**.

Step 1: Install the Debug Toolbar

sh
CopyEdit

```
pip install django-debug-toolbar
```

Step 2: Add It to INSTALLED_APPS in settings.py

python
CopyEdit

```
INSTALLED_APPS += ["debug_toolbar"]
```

Step 3: Update Middleware and URLs

Modify settings.py:

python
CopyEdit

```
MIDDLEWARE += ["debug_toolbar.middleware.DebugToolbarMiddleware"]
```

```
INTERNAL_IPS = ["127.0.0.1"]
```

Modify urls.py:

python
CopyEdit
```
from django.urls import include, path

urlpatterns = [
    path("__debug__/", include("debug_toolbar.urls")),
]
```

■ **Now, queries executed by Django ORM appear in the debug toolbar.**

1.3 Optimizing Queries with select_related() and prefetch_related()

Django's ORM uses **lazy loading**, meaning every related object triggers a **separate SQL query**. This can be slow when fetching related models.

Bad Practice: Causing N+1 Queries

python
CopyEdit
```
for order in Order.objects.all():
    print(order.customer.name)  # This causes multiple queries
```

■ **Optimized Query Using select_related()**

python
CopyEdit
```
orders = Order.objects.select_related("customer").all()
for order in orders:
    print(order.customer.name)  # Only one query is executed
```

343

■ Use prefetch_related() for Many-to-Many Relationships

python
CopyEdit
```python
products = Product.objects.prefetch_related("categories").all()
```

1.4 Using Database Indexing for Faster Queries

Indexes **speed up search queries** by reducing the number of rows scanned.
■ Django automatically creates indexes for primary and foreign keys, but additional indexes may be needed.

Modify models.py:

python
CopyEdit
```python
class Product(models.Model):
    name = models.CharField(max_length=255, db_index=True)  # Indexed for faster lookups
    price = models.DecimalField(max_digits=10, decimal_places=2)
```

■ Now, searching for a product by name runs faster.

1.5 Efficient Query Filtering

Avoid inefficient queries:

python
CopyEdit
```python
products = Product.objects.all()  # Retrieves all products (slow)
filtered_products = [p for p in products if p.price > 50]  # Filtering in Python (slow)
```

■ Filter data at the database level:

python
CopyEdit
```python
products = Product.objects.filter(price__gt=50)  # SQL executes filtering (fast)
```

344

Using Caching for Faster Performance (Redis, Memcached)

Caching stores **frequently accessed data in memory**, reducing database hits and improving performance. Django supports **multiple caching backends**, including **Redis and Memcached**.

2.1 Configuring Django's Built-In Caching

Modify settings.py to enable caching:

```python
CopyEdit
CACHES = {
    "default": {
        "BACKEND": "django.core.cache.backends.locmem.LocMemCache",
        "LOCATION": "unique-snowflake",
    }
}
```

🔲 **Django now stores cached data in local memory.**

2.2 Using Redis for High-Performance Caching

Redis is a **fast in-memory cache** that outperforms **file-based or database caching**.

Step 1: Install Redis and Django Redis Package

```sh
CopyEdit
sudo apt install redis
pip install django-redis
```

Step 2: Configure Redis in settings.py

python
CopyEdit
```
CACHES = {
  "default": {
    "BACKEND": "django.core.cache.backends.redis.RedisCache",
    "LOCATION": "redis://127.0.0.1:6379/1",
  }
}
```

■ **Now, Django stores cache data in Redis.**

2.3 Caching Expensive Database Queries

Some queries **don't change often** and should be cached.

Modify views.py:

python
CopyEdit
```
from django.core.cache import cache

def get_top_products():
    cached_products = cache.get("top_products")
    if cached_products is None:
        cached_products = Product.objects.order_by("-sales")[:10]
        cache.set("top_products", cached_products, timeout=300)  # Cache for 5 minutes
    return cached_products
```

■ **Django avoids repeated database queries by storing the result in Redis.**

2.4 Caching Views for Faster Responses

Django allows **entire views** to be cached.

Modify views.py:

python
CopyEdit
```python
from django.views.decorators.cache import cache_page

@cache_page(60 * 15)  # Cache page for 15 minutes
def product_list(request):
    products = Product.objects.all()
    return render(request, "products.html", {"products": products})
```

■ **Subsequent requests serve data from cache instead of hitting the database.**

2.5 Using Memcached for Distributed Caching

Memcached is a **lightweight and fast caching system** for handling **high-volume data requests**.

Step 1: Install Memcached and Django Package
sh
CopyEdit
```sh
sudo apt install memcached
pip install python-memcached
```

Step 2: Configure Memcached in settings.py
python
CopyEdit
```python
CACHES = {
    "default": {
        "BACKEND": "django.core.cache.backends.memcached.PyMemcacheCache",
        "LOCATION": "127.0.0.1:11211",
    }
}
```

■ **Now, Django stores cached data in Memcached.**

347

2.6 Fragment Caching (Partially Caching Templates)

Sometimes, **only part of a page** should be cached.

Modify product_list.html:

html
CopyEdit
```
{% load cache %}
{% cache 300 product_section %}
  <ul>
    {% for product in products %}
      <li>{{ product.name }} - ${{ product.price }}</li>
    {% endfor %}
  </ul>
{% endcache %}
```

■ **Only the product section is cached, not the entire page.**

Load Balancing and Scaling Django Apps

1.1 What is Load Balancing?

Load balancing distributes incoming traffic across **multiple Django servers**, preventing **overloading** of a single server and improving availability.

■ **Without Load Balancing:**

- A single Django server handles all requests.
- **High traffic leads to slow performance or crashes.**

■ **With Load Balancing:**

- Requests are evenly spread across multiple servers.
- **Prevents overloading and improves fault tolerance.**

1.2 Setting Up a Load Balancer with Nginx

Nginx is a popular choice for **Django load balancing**. It distributes traffic between multiple Django application servers.

Step 1: Install Nginx

sh

CopyEdit

```
sudo apt update
sudo apt install nginx
```

Step 2: Configure Load Balancing in Nginx

Modify the Nginx configuration file (e.g., /etc/nginx/sites-available/django):

nginx

CopyEdit

```
upstream django_servers {
    server 127.0.0.1:8001;  # First Django server
    server 127.0.0.1:8002;  # Second Django server
}

server {
    listen 80;
    server_name yourdomain.com;

    location / {
```

```
proxy_pass http://django_servers;

proxy_set_header Host $host;

proxy_set_header X-Real-IP $remote_addr;

proxy_set_header X-Forwarded-For $proxy_add_x_forwarded_for;

    }

}
```

Step 3: Restart Nginx

sh

CopyEdit

```
sudo systemctl restart nginx
```

■ **Now, Nginx distributes incoming requests across multiple Django servers.**

1.3 Running Multiple Django Instances with Gunicorn

Django typically runs on a **single process**, but multiple instances can be started for load balancing.

Step 1: Install Gunicorn

sh

CopyEdit

```
pip install gunicorn
```

Step 2: Run Multiple Django Servers

sh

CopyEdit

```
gunicorn --workers=3 --bind=127.0.0.1:8001 myproject.wsgi:application &
gunicorn --workers=3 --bind=127.0.0.1:8002 myproject.wsgi:application &
```

■ **Now, Nginx distributes traffic across multiple Gunicorn instances.**

1.4 Scaling Django with AWS Elastic Load Balancer (ELB)

For **cloud deployments**, AWS provides **Elastic Load Balancer (ELB)** to distribute traffic automatically.

Step 1: Deploy Django on Multiple EC2 Instances

- Launch **two or more EC2 instances** running Django.
- Connect each instance to **a shared database (RDS, PostgreSQL, etc.)**.

Step 2: Set Up Elastic Load Balancer (ELB)

1. Go to **AWS Management Console** → EC2 → Load Balancers.
2. Click **Create Load Balancer** and select **Application Load Balancer**.
3. Add Django servers to the **Target Group**.
4. Configure **HTTP to HTTPS redirection** for secure connections.

■ **AWS ELB automatically distributes traffic across Django instances.**

Handling High Traffic with Asynchronous Django

Django traditionally follows a **synchronous request-response model**, meaning each request is handled sequentially. However, high-traffic applications **benefit from asynchronous processing**.

2.1 Using Asynchronous Django Views (Django 3.1+)

Django 3.1 introduced **async views,** allowing non-blocking request handling.

Example: Traditional Blocking View

python

CopyEdit

```python
from django.http import JsonResponse
import time


def slow_view(request):
    time.sleep(5)  # Simulates a long-running process
    return JsonResponse({"message": "Response after 5 seconds"})
```

⏳ **Issue**: Requests **block** the server until the response is sent.

Example: Asynchronous View (Non-Blocking)

python

CopyEdit

```python
from django.http import JsonResponse
import asyncio


async def async_slow_view(request):
    await asyncio.sleep(5)  # Non-blocking sleep
```

```python
return JsonResponse({"message": "Async response after 5 seconds"})
```

■ **Now, Django can handle other requests while waiting.**

2.2 Background Processing with Celery and Redis

For tasks that **shouldn't block user requests**, Celery can process them in the background.

Step 1: Install Celery and Redis

sh

CopyEdit

```sh
pip install celery redis
sudo apt install redis
```

Step 2: Configure Celery in Django (celery.py)

Modify celery.py in the Django project:

python

CopyEdit

```python
from celery import Celery


app = Celery("myproject")
app.config_from_object("django.conf:settings", namespace="CELERY")
app.autodiscover_tasks()
```

Modify settings.py:

python

CopyEdit

CELERY_BROKER_URL = "redis://localhost:6379/0"

2.3 Creating an Asynchronous Task with Celery

Modify tasks.py inside a Django app:

python

CopyEdit

```
from celery import shared_task
import time


@shared_task
def process_large_file():
    time.sleep(10)
    return "File processed successfully"
```

■ Now, tasks run in the background instead of blocking the request.

2.4 Running Celery Workers

Start a Celery worker to process tasks:

sh

CopyEdit

```
celery -A myproject worker --loglevel=info
```

⬛ Now, tasks are handled asynchronously, improving Django's response time.

2.5 Using Django Channels for Real-Time Applications

Django Channels enables **real-time features like notifications, chat, and live updates**.

Step 1: Install Django Channels

sh

CopyEdit

```
pip install channels
```

Step 2: Configure ASGI in settings.py

python

CopyEdit

```
ASGI_APPLICATION = "myproject.asgi.application"

CHANNEL_LAYERS = {
    "default": {
```

```
        "BACKEND": "channels.layers.InMemoryChannelLayer",

    }

}
```

2.6 Creating a Real-Time WebSocket Consumer

Modify consumers.py:

python

CopyEdit

```python
import json

from channels.generic.websocket import AsyncWebsocketConsumer


class ChatConsumer(AsyncWebsocketConsumer):
    async def connect(self):
        await self.accept()

    async def disconnect(self, close_code):
        pass

    async def receive(self, text_data):
        data = json.loads(text_data)
        await self.send(text_data=json.dumps({"message": data["message"]}))
```

■ Now, Django handles real-time WebSocket connections asynchronously.

Chapter 16: Final Thoughts and Next Steps

As we reach the conclusion of this book, it's essential to reflect on the **key takeaways** and discuss how to stay **up to date with Django's future releases**. The world of web development evolves rapidly, and Django continues to improve, offering better performance, enhanced security, and new features with each version.

Summary of Key Takeaways

Throughout this book, we explored Django's capabilities **from basic concepts to advanced real-world applications**. Let's summarize the most crucial lessons:

1.1 Understanding Django's Core Architecture

■ **MTV Pattern (Model-Template-View)** – Django follows a structured pattern that separates **database models, views (logic), and templates (UI)**.
■ **Django's App-Based Structure** – Applications within a Django project are modular and reusable.

1.2 Building Django Web Applications

■ **Models and Django ORM** – Define database structures using models and interact with them using **Django ORM**.
■ **Views and URL Routing** – Handle HTTP requests with **Function-Based Views (FBVs)** or **Class-Based Views (CBVs)**.
■ **Templates and Static Files** – Use **Django Template Language (DTL)** to render dynamic content efficiently.

1.3 User Authentication and Security Best Practices

■ **Django's Built-in Authentication System** – Secure user login, registration, and password management.
■ **Customizing Authentication** – Modify the **User model** to fit specific application needs.
■ **Securing Django Apps** – Use **CSRF protection, XSS prevention, and SQL injection safeguards** to enhance security.

1.4 Django REST Framework (DRF) and API Development

■ **Building RESTful APIs** – Use Django REST Framework (DRF) to create APIs for mobile and frontend applications.
■ **Serialization and API Views** – Transform Django models into JSON responses.
■ **API Authentication** – Secure APIs using **Token-based authentication, JWT, or OAuth**.

1.5 Advanced Django Features

■ **Django Channels** – Implement **real-time WebSockets** for chat applications, live notifications, and real-time dashboards.
■ **Multi-Tenancy with Django** – Use django-tenants or tenant_id **filtering** for SaaS applications.
■ **Django with AI** – Integrate **OpenAI's GPT, TensorFlow, or Scikit-Learn** for machine learning applications.

1.6 Performance Optimization and Scalability

■ **Database Query Optimization** – Reduce **N+1 queries** with select_related() and prefetch_related().
■ **Caching for Faster Performance** – Implement caching with **Redis, Memcached, and Django's built-in cache**.
■ **Load Balancing and Scaling** – Distribute traffic across multiple Django instances using **Nginx, Gunicorn, and AWS Elastic Load Balancer (ELB)**.
■ **Asynchronous Django** – Use **Celery for background tasks** and **Django Channels for real-time features**.

1.7 Deployment and Cloud Integration

■ **Deploying Django on AWS, Heroku, or DigitalOcean** – Use **Gunicorn, Nginx, and Docker** for efficient deployment.
■ **Using Docker and Kubernetes** – Containerize Django applications for **scalable and portable** cloud environments.
■ **Setting Up CI/CD Pipelines** – Automate deployments using **GitHub Actions, GitLab CI, or Jenkins**.

Staying Updated with Django's Future Releases

Django's ecosystem **continually evolves**, with new features, security patches, and optimizations being introduced in each version. To **stay relevant and improve your Django skills**, follow these best practices:

2.1 Following Django's Official Roadmap

Django has an official **release cycle** with updates every **8-12 months**. You can track progress via:

- **Official Django Website** – https://www.djangoproject.com
- **Django's GitHub Repository** – https://github.com/django/django
- **Django's Release Notes** – Stay informed about **new features, bug fixes, and deprecations** in each version.

■ Best Practice: Always **test new Django versions in a staging environment** before upgrading production systems.

2.2 Engaging with the Django Community

The **Django community** is one of the most active in web development. Engaging with the community helps you **stay updated, troubleshoot issues, and learn new best practices**.

- **Django Forum** – https://forum.djangoproject.com
- **Stack Overflow** – https://stackoverflow.com/questions/tagged/django
- **Django Discord Channel** – A great place for discussions and live support.

■ Best Practice: Contribute to open-source Django projects and **help beginners** in forums to reinforce your knowledge.

2.3 Reading Django Blogs and Tutorials

Many industry professionals write about Django updates, new features, and best practices. Some reliable sources include:

- **Django News** – https://django-news.com
- **Real Python's Django Tutorials** – https://realpython.com/tutorials/django/
- **TestDriven.io** – Covers Django **API development, testing, and deployments**.

Best Practice: Subscribe to **Django newsletters** and follow developers on **Twitter, LinkedIn, and Medium.**

2.4 Experimenting with New Django Features

As Django evolves, it introduces **new features like async support, query optimizations, and security enhancements.**

Best Practice: Create **side projects** to test new Django releases before integrating them into production applications.

Example:

1. Set up a **Docker container** with multiple Django versions for testing.
2. Use **feature flags** to selectively enable new features in production.
3. Regularly **review Django's deprecation warnings** to future-proof your codebase.

2.5 Learning Related Technologies

Django is a **full-stack web framework**, but **mastering complementary tools** makes you a better developer.

* **Frontend Frameworks** – Learn **React, Vue.js, or HTMX** for better Django-frontend integration.
* **Databases** – Understand **PostgreSQL, MySQL, and NoSQL databases like MongoDB.**
* **DevOps** – Get familiar with **Docker, Kubernetes, AWS, and CI/CD pipelines.**

Best Practice: Stay **curious** and **expand your knowledge** beyond Django to become a well-rounded developer.

Final Thoughts

Django is a **powerful and versatile web framework** that enables developers to build **scalable, secure, and efficient applications.** Whether you're a beginner learning Django for the first time or an experienced developer optimizing large-scale applications, Django offers the tools and flexibility needed to succeed.

By continuously **learning, engaging with the community, and staying up to date with new releases**, you can master Django and build high-performance web applications that stand the test of time.

This book has equipped you with **comprehensive Django knowledge**—from fundamental concepts to advanced real-world implementations. Now, it's time to **apply what you've learned and build something amazing!**

Next Steps: What to Do Now?

■ **Revisit Chapters & Implement Concepts** – Pick sections that interest you and build small projects.
■ **Work on Real Django Projects** – Create SaaS apps, REST APIs, or AI-powered Django applications.
■ **Contribute to Open Source** – Join Django's open-source projects on GitHub.
■ **Stay Curious & Keep Learning** – Follow the latest Django trends and explore new features.

Thank You for Reading!

You now have everything needed to **build, optimize, and scale Django applications**. Keep experimenting, stay engaged with the Django community, and most importantly—**keep coding!**

As you continue your journey with Django, the next steps involve **expanding your knowledge, building a portfolio, and contributing to open-source projects**. This will not only **strengthen your expertise** but also **help you stand out as a Django developer**.

Recommended Resources for Further Learning

1.1 Django's Official Documentation

The **Django documentation** is the best place to **stay updated on new features, best practices, and official guidelines**.

- **Website**: https://docs.djangoproject.com/en/stable/

■ **Best Practice:** Read the release notes **before upgrading Django** to avoid breaking changes in your projects.

1.2 Books on Django

If you prefer structured learning, these books provide **in-depth Django knowledge**:

🍲 **Two Scoops of Django** – Covers **best practices for Django development**.
🍲 **Django for Professionals** – Teaches **scalable and secure Django development**.
🍲 **Test-Driven Development with Django** – Focuses on **writing better code with automated tests**.

■ **Best Practice:** Choose a book that matches your level (**beginner, intermediate, or advanced**) and follow along with **hands-on projects**.

1.3 Online Django Courses

If you prefer **video tutorials**, these platforms offer high-quality Django courses:

🎥 **Udemy:** "Python Django – The Practical Guide"
🎥 **Coursera:** "Django for Everybody" by the University of Michigan
🎥 **Real Python:** Advanced Django tutorials and deep dives
🎥 **TestDriven.io:** Covers **Django REST Framework, APIs, and testing**

■ **Best Practice:** Enroll in **one course at a time** and apply concepts in **small projects**.

1.4 Django Blogs, Podcasts, and Newsletters

Staying updated on Django trends helps you **learn about new techniques and tools**.

- **Django News** – Weekly updates on Django releases, tutorials, and jobs.
- **Real Python Blog** – Covers Django, Python, and web development best practices.
- **Talk Python to Me (Podcast)** – Interviews with Django and Python experts.

■ **Best Practice:** Subscribe to Django newsletters and **read one technical blog per week**.

Building Your Own Django Portfolio

A **strong Django portfolio** showcases your **skills, experience, and problem-solving abilities**. Whether you're applying for a job, freelancing, or launching your startup, a portfolio helps demonstrate your **expertise in Django development**.

2.1 What to Include in Your Django Portfolio?

■ **Real-World Django Projects** – Applications that solve real problems.
■ **API Development** – Show your experience with **Django REST Framework (DRF)**.
■ **Frontend Integration** – Combine Django with **React, Vue.js, or HTMX**.
■ **Optimized and Scalable Code** – Show how you handle **performance and security**.
■ **Deployment Experience** – List your experience with **AWS, Docker, Heroku, or DigitalOcean**.

2.2 Sample Django Portfolio Projects

- ◆ **A Personal Blog or Portfolio Website** – Showcases your work and writing skills.
- ◆ **E-Commerce Platform** – Includes **product management, authentication, and payment integration**.
- ◆ **Task Manager with Django and React** – Displays API and frontend integration skills.
- ◆ **AI-Powered Django App** – Uses **OpenAI, TensorFlow, or NLP for intelligent features**.
- ◆ **Multi-Tenant SaaS App** – Demonstrates **advanced database design**.

■ **Best Practice:** Host projects on **GitHub**, deploy them online, and write a **technical blog** explaining each project.

2.3 How to Present Your Django Portfolio?

1. **GitHub Repository** – Keep your code clean, structured, and well-documented.
2. **Live Demo Link** – Deploy your project using **Heroku, AWS, or DigitalOcean**.
3. **Project Write-Up** – Explain your tech stack, architecture, and challenges faced.
4. **Personal Website** – Use Django to **build your own portfolio site** with case studies.

■ **Best Practice: Make your portfolio interactive** – allow visitors to sign up, interact with the features, and test your applications.

Contributing to Open Source

Contributing to **open-source Django projects** helps you:
■ Improve your coding skills by working with experienced developers.
■ Build a **strong reputation** in the Django community.
■ Gain **real-world experience** and showcase your contributions on GitHub.

3.1 How to Get Started with Open Source Contributions?

◆ **Step 1: Find Beginner-Friendly Issues** – Start with **small bug fixes** or documentation updates.
◆ **Step 2: Read the Contribution Guidelines** – Each project has **rules for contributing**.
◆ **Step 3: Fork the Repository and Fix an Issue** – Create a branch, fix the issue, and submit a Pull Request (PR).
◆ **Step 4: Engage with the Community** – Join Django's **mailing lists, forums, and Discord channels**.

■ **Best Practice:** Contribute to projects that **align with your interests** (e.g., Django core, Django REST Framework, or open-source SaaS projects).

3.2 Where to Find Open-Source Django Projects?

1. **Django's Official GitHub Repository** – https://github.com/django/django
2. **Django REST Framework** – https://github.com/encode/django-rest-framework
3. **Awesome Django Projects** – https://github.com/wsvincent/awesome-django
4. **First Contributions** – A beginner-friendly open-source project.

■ **Best Practice:** Start with **documentation fixes**, then progress to **bug fixes and feature contributions**.

3.3 How Open-Source Contributions Help Your Career

■ **Enhances Your Resume** – Employers value real-world coding experience.
■ **Builds Your Network** – Engage with experienced Django developers.
■ **Increases Your Job Prospects** – Open-source contributors stand out in hiring processes.

■ **Best Practice:** List your **open-source contributions** in your **portfolio and LinkedIn profile** to attract job opportunities.

Final Words: Keep Learning and Keep Building!

At this point, you have a **solid foundation** in Django and the tools to build and scale real-world applications. But **learning never stops!**

■ **Set new goals** – Aim to build a **new Django project every 3-6 months**.
■ **Stay active in the Django community** – Engage in **forums, conferences, and open-source projects**.
■ **Learn new technologies** – Explore **AI, DevOps, Frontend, and cloud deployments** to enhance your Django skills.

Django is a **powerful, scalable, and versatile framework**, and by continuously improving your skills, you'll become a **top-tier Django developer** in no time.

What's Next?

* **Build your next Django project.**
* **Publish a technical blog on Medium or Dev.to.**
* **Contribute to an open-source Django project.**
* **Join a Django meetup or conference.**

💡 **Remember:** The best way to learn **is to build!** 🚀

Thank You for Reading! Happy Coding with Django!

Appendices

This section provides **quick references, solutions to common Django errors, essential commands, and useful resources** for Django developers.

Appendix A: Common Django Errors and Fixes

Even experienced Django developers encounter errors. Here's a list of **common Django issues and how to fix them**.

1. ImportError: No module named Django

■ **Cause:** Django is not installed or the virtual environment is not activated.

■ **Solution:**

```sh
CopyEdit
pip install django
# Or activate your virtual environment first:
source venv/bin/activate  # macOS/Linux
venv\Scripts\activate    # Windows
```

2. ImproperlyConfigured: settings.py Not Found

■ **Cause:** Django cannot locate the settings module.

■ **Solution:** Ensure you set the environment variable correctly:

```sh
CopyEdit
export DJANGO_SETTINGS_MODULE=myproject.settings  # macOS/Linux
set DJANGO_SETTINGS_MODULE=myproject.settings    # Windows
```

Or explicitly define it in manage.py:

```python
import os
os.environ.setdefault("DJANGO_SETTINGS_MODULE", "myproject.settings")
```

3. TemplateDoesNotExist Error

■ **Cause:** Django cannot find the template file.

■ **Solution:**

- Ensure the template is located in a **registered** directory.
- Update settings.py:

```python
TEMPLATES = [
    {
        "BACKEND": "django.template.backends.django.DjangoTemplates",
        "DIRS": [BASE_DIR / "templates"],  # Ensure this path is correct
    },
]
```

4. NoReverseMatch Error

■ **Cause:** The URL name used in {% url 'name' %} or reverse('name') does not exist.

■ **Solution:**

- Verify URL patterns in urls.py.
- Ensure correct **namespace** is used in {% url 'app_name:view_name' %} if applicable.

5. ModuleNotFoundError: No module named 'app_name'

■ **Cause:** The Django app is missing from INSTALLED_APPS.

■ **Solution:** Add the app to INSTALLED_APPS in settings.py:

python
CopyEdit
```python
INSTALLED_APPS = [
    "myapp",
]
```

6. CSRF Token Missing or Incorrect

■ **Cause:** CSRF protection is enabled, but the token is missing from the request.

■ **Solution:** Ensure all **POST** forms include {% csrf_token %}:

html
CopyEdit
```html
<form method="POST">
    {% csrf_token %}
    <input type="text" name="username">
</form>
```

For **AJAX requests**, pass the CSRF token in headers:

javascript
CopyEdit
```javascript
fetch('/api/', {
    method: 'POST',
    headers: {
        'X-CSRFToken': getCookie('csrftoken'),
        'Content-Type': 'application/json'
    },
    body: JSON.stringify(data)
});
```

369

7. IntegrityError: UNIQUE constraint failed

■ **Cause:** A field marked as unique=True is receiving duplicate values.

■ **Solution:**

- Ensure **data validation** before saving new records.
- Use get_or_create() instead of create():

python
CopyEdit
```
user, created = User.objects.get_or_create(email="test@example.com")
```

8. Django Admin Login Not Working

■ **Cause:** The superuser account may not exist.

■ **Solution:** Create a new superuser:

sh
CopyEdit
```
python manage.py createsuperuser
```

Then restart the development server:

sh
CopyEdit
```
python manage.py runserver
```

9. Database Migration Errors

■ **Cause:** Migrations are missing or out of sync.

■ **Solution:**

sh
CopyEdit
```
python manage.py makemigrations
python manage.py migrate --fake-initial  # If initial migrations fail
```

If issues persist, reset migrations:

sh
CopyEdit
```
rm -rf myapp/migrations
python manage.py makemigrations
python manage.py migrate
```

10. Static Files Not Loading in Production

■ **Cause:** Django is not correctly serving static files.

■ **Solution:**

- Ensure **STATICFILES_DIRS** is set in settings.py:

python
CopyEdit
```
STATIC_URL = "/static/"
STATICFILES_DIRS = [BASE_DIR / "static"]
STATIC_ROOT = BASE_DIR / "staticfiles"
```

- Run **collectstatic**:

sh
CopyEdit
```
python manage.py collectstatic
```

- In **production**, configure Nginx or Apache to serve static files.

Appendix B: Django Cheat Sheet (Quick Commands and Shortcuts)

1. Virtual Environment Management

sh

CopyEdit

```
python -m venv venv     # Create a virtual environment
source venv/bin/activate # Activate (macOS/Linux)
venv\Scripts\activate   # Activate (Windows)
deactivate              # Deactivate
```

2. Creating a Django Project and App

sh

CopyEdit

```
django-admin startproject myproject  # Create project
cd myproject
python manage.py startapp myapp      # Create app
```

3. Running the Development Server

sh

CopyEdit

```
python manage.py runserver
python manage.py runserver 0.0.0.0:8000  # Allow external access
```

4. Managing the Database

sh

CopyEdit

```
python manage.py makemigrations # Create migration files
```

```sh
python manage.py migrate      # Apply migrations
python manage.py dbshell      # Open database shell
```

5. Creating a Superuser

sh
CopyEdit

```sh
python manage.py createsuperuser
```

6. Working with the Django Shell

sh
CopyEdit

```sh
python manage.py shell
```

Inside the shell:

python
CopyEdit

```python
from myapp.models import User
User.objects.all()
```

7. Using the Django Admin Panel

sh
CopyEdit

```sh
python manage.py createsuperuser
```

Then login at:
📌 **http://127.0.0.1:8000/admin/**

8. Running Tests

sh
CopyEdit

```
python manage.py test myapp
```

9. Collecting Static Files for Production

sh
CopyEdit

```
python manage.py collectstatic
```

Appendix C: Resources for Django Developers

Official Django Resources

* **Django Documentation** – https://docs.djangoproject.com/
* **Django GitHub Repository** – https://github.com/django/django
* **Django Community Forum** – https://forum.djangoproject.com/

Best Django Blogs & Tutorials

📌 **Real Python Django Tutorials** – https://realpython.com/tutorials/django/
📌 **Django News** – https://django-news.com
📌 **Simple is Better Than Complex** – https://simpleisbetterthancomplex.com/

Django Communities & Support

📌 **Stack Overflow** – https://stackoverflow.com/questions/tagged/django
📌 **Django Discord Server** – https://discord.com/invite/django
📌 **Reddit Django Community** – https://www.reddit.com/r/django/

Advanced Django Courses & Books

● **Two Scoops of Django** – Best practices for Django developers.
● **Django for Professionals** – Covers advanced Django topics like deployment and security.
● **Test-Driven Development with Django** – A deep dive into testing Django apps.

Django Deployment & DevOps

📌 **Deploy Django with Docker** – https://testdriven.io/blog/dockerizing-django/
📌 **Scaling Django with AWS** –
https://realpython.com/deploying-a-django-app-and-postgresql-to-aws/

Final Words

With these **quick references, troubleshooting tips, and resources**, you now have everything needed to **build, optimize, and deploy Django applications like a pro**.

Keep learning, keep building, and stay active in the Django community!